THE LIFE

FRANCI

THE MEX_ _ _ _ _ _ _ _

BY CAPT' KENNEDY U. S. A.

NO. 9

**A TRUE AND AUTHENTIC LIFE HISTORY OF THE MOST
NOTED BANDIT THAT EVER LIVED. A MAN
WHO HAS OVERTHROWN THE
GOVERNMENT OF MEX-
ICO AND DEFIED
THE UNITED
STATES.**

I. & M. OTTENHEIMER,
Publishers
321 W. BALTIMORE ST.
BALTIMORE, MD.

FRANCISCO VILLA
THE MEXICAN BANBIT.

CHAPTER I.

Thirty-seven years ago there was born a man who was destined to shock by his deeds the civilized world.

He has been known through the terrible days of his life of robbery, arson and murder as Francisco Villa.

But that was not the name under which he was christened by the priest in the little mountain town of Las Nieves, in the State of Durango, Mexico.

That name was Doroteo Arranzo.

What caused him to take the name of Francisco

Villa, and to bestow it upon his family is, apparently, known only to himself and so far as authentic records show he has never offered any explanation.

Indeed, the whole history of his birth, even of his parentage, is shrouded in mystery.

As to who his father was, accounts differ. Some say that he was a negro, others that he was of Mexican origin.

Villa's mother, however, was a full-blooded Indian.

Besides the notorious bandit, there was born to the Arranzos, or Villas as they are now known, a daughter.

In her were embodied all the traits of her parents and to them she added a beauty so unusual that she was courted by Mexicans from far and near.

Villa loved his sister passionately and it was because of her that he became an outlaw and was forced to live in the bush, prize money mounting into the thousands on his head, hunted relentlessly by the Rurales —or mounted police—for fifteen years.

Of the early days of the bandit's life little is known. But we may suppose he grew up on the little ranch owned by his family.

He is said to have received a most pious training at 'the hands of a priest.

The fact remains, however, that Villa is grossly

illiterate, can neither read nor write, but has learned to sign his name.

When authentic history first takes cognizance of Doroteo Arranzo he was eighteen years old.

At the time, he was known as Francisco Villa, and was busily engaged in cultivating the 50 acres which constituted the Villa ranch in Las Nieves.

In stature he was of medium height, with massive shoulders and what has been called a perfect "bullet-shaped" head.

His eyes were brown and he had a mustache which did not hide the noticeable ugliness of his mouth, an ugliness enhanced by the fact that his teeth were yellow and irregular.

His garb consisted of cotton trousers, cotton shirt and the pointed sombrero.

Money, of which he has always been so covetous, from the day he took up his life of outlawry, was almost unknown to him.

It is said that he saved what he earned for two years before he had enough to buy his first gun.

But, apparently, almost as soon as he got it he used it to commit murder, for he was but twenty years old when he killed his first man.

And the money to buy this gun was earned by Villa by driving cattle owned by neighboring ranchers over the mountain to be sold.

History records another member of the Villa family in those days in the person of an aged grandparent.

The killing of his first man sent Villa to the mountains as an outlaw.

At that time, when he was but twenty years old, began the hunt for him which lasted for fifteen years.

During this period, he robbed, burned and murdered till his name became a terror throughout the length and breadth of Mexico.

Never was there a day when the Rurales were not on his trail. But he seemed to bear a charmed life, a superstition which he has always been at the greatest pains to inculcate in the minds of his ignorant fellow-country men.

No matter how clever the traps laid for him, he always managed to extricate himself: no matter how overwhelming the odds against him, he always managed to escape.

Nine times he was wounded but from them all he recovered.

Each act of crime he committed made him bolder. He rode about the country fearlessly, helping himself to anything he wanted, killing those who incurred his anger or his ever-excitable suspicion, till in desperation, Porfirio Diaz, then president of Mexico, offered a reward of twenty thousand dollars for his capture.

But even this prize money, great as it was to the people among whom he lived, did not induce any one to kill him, though many tried.

Upon Francisco Madero, for a while president of Mexico, the onus of transforming Villa from a terror-inspiring bandit to a national hero is placed.

During the latter part of the fifteen years when he was nothing but a desperate outlaw, Villa made the acquaintance of Raoul Madero, brother of Francisco.

At the time, Francisco was pushing his revolt against the rule of Porfirio Diaz.

The bandit seemed to fascinate Raoul and they became great chums.

As the Madero revolution vacillated between failure and success, finally seeming doomed to failure, Raoul Madero conceived the idea of enlisting Villa in his brother's cause.

Sometime during his career, the bandit is said to have served in the United States Army.

At all events, he had a crude knowledge of affairs military, and Raoul was impressed with the manner in which he inspired blind devotion on the part of his followers.

Having conceived the idea, Raoul wrote to his brother. There is said to be a letter on record in which Raoul extols the bandit as a hero and genius at the very time when he was feared throughout Mexico as a blood-lusting cut-throat.

Willing to grasp at any straw that might save the day for his fast-failing revolution, Francisco Madero sent a commission to the bandit.

From that day when, as a soldier, he took up arms against the rule of Porfirio Diaz, Villa's deeds have alternately horrified and roused the admiration of the entire world.

The men whom Villa gathered into his command worshipped him.

To all his followers he has always been "Pancho"— the Spanish nickname for Francisco—evidence that they knew and felt that he was one of their own mould, not a member of the hated aristocracy or land-owning class.

In the days of his outlawry, he was dubbed "The Tiger."

When he became an officer in the revolutionary army of Francisco Madero he declared himself to be the people's idol and terror—and he still is today among the masses of the Mexicans.

When Diaz was at last deposed and Madero became president with Victoriano Huerta as his generalissimo, there sprang up the same intense hatred between Villa and Huerta that had existed between Villa and Diaz.

Huerta cast Villa into jail.

Madero quickly released him.

But when Huerta ascended to the presidency after Madero's death, one of his first acts was to cast Villa into jail again.

His luck still held true, however, and before Huerta could have him removed "Pancho" escaped.

As might be expected, no sooner had he made his escape than the people's idol and terror took up arms against Huerta.

CHAPTER II.

VILLA'S FIRST MURDER.

It is not the purpose in this story of Francisco Villa to narrate his deeds since he became a revolutionist—the newspapers and magazines have chronicled his movements and exploits from the day he went to Madero's aid—but to give the account of the obscure days when he terrorized his native land by his outlawry.

But it will give an insight into this man whose followers acclaim him as hero and whose enemies call him the devil incarnate, to consider his characteristics.

From his Indian mother he received his violent emotion, either for love or hate, his superstition, his marvellous agility and his suspicion.

From his father he doubtless inherited his love for drink, for women, and his fearlessness.

Because of his lowly origin, the ignorant masses of the Mexicans feel and know that he is one of them and they yield to him blind obedience.

He seems to have a marvellous faculty of attracting men of all ranks and descriptions to him and his ability to handle his men and to direct his armies has led some of his most enthusiastic admirers and apologists to place him high upon the pinnacle of fame as a military genius.

But despite the glory and honors that have been accorded him, Francisco Villa is a murderer and was for fifteen years before he acquired fame as a soldier.

To those who delight to place the blame for a man's mistakes and crimes upon a woman, there will be a cynical satisfaction that the woman in Villa's case was his sister.

As has been said, her beauty made her the toast throughout the State of Durango.

Among the innumerable wooers who serenaded her with their guitars or chatted with her as they lazily puffed their cigarettes, was the sheriff, or *jefe politico*.

Whether it was his rank or his personality, it soon became evident to her other suitors and to her family, that the sheriff had her preference.

It is evident that Villa viewed this attachment between a man of high standing in the State and his humble, though beautiful, sister with suspicion.

At last his opposition to the courtship became so pronounced that when Villa went on one of his trips across the mountains with cattle for one of his neighbors, the sheriff and the girl took advantage of his absence to elope.

Evidently fearing some such event, Villa had commissioned one of his chums, Dato Lopez, to keep his eye on the lovers.

When they eloped, Dato rode post haste to inform Villa.

"Were they married?" demanded the brother, as his chum finished his story.

"There are no records of any ceremony," Dato replied.

Crazed by the information, Villa turned over the driving of the cattle to market to a cowboy and rode back to Las Nieves with Dato.

Arrived, he hurriedly enlisted two other friends to help him in the plan he had formed as he rode home to his little ranch, Bepo and Enrico.

Accompanied by them, he went to the village priest.

"Father," said he, "I want you to go into the mountains with me to marry my sister to the sheriff."

Deeming refusal dangerous, the priest agreed and quickly were they under way.

Without difficulty, Villa picked up the trail of the elopers and when he reached the last ranch house before entering the mountains he borrowed a spade.

Three days' hard riding brought them just at sundown to the spot where the elopers had pitched their camp.

They were away when the little troop arrived but soon returned.

At the sight of the brother with whose sister he had run away, the sheriff stopped, then looked about for a means of escape.

"Don't run, come here!" thundered Villa, covering the official with his gun, the gun to buy which he had saved for two years.

Unwillingly the couple obeyed.

"Are you married?" Villa demanded of his sister.

But she only hung her head.

"Answer me!" he roared, his eyes wild with fury.

Still his sister kept silent, cowering for protection against the man with whom she eloped.

"I know you are not. If you were, you would tell me. But before the sun sets tonight you will be," he growled.

"Only a priest can marry us," exclaimed the sheriff, thinking he had found a way to avoid the ceremony with the low-caste beauty.

"And only a priest will," snarled Villa.

"But how can we be married before sunset if there is no priest?" demanded the sheriff.

"I have brought one," the brother answered. Then turning to his companions, he said: "Bepo, ask the good father to come here."

For Villa had deemed it wise to conceal the presence of the priest by hiding him behind a rock.

As the good father stepped forth, the sheriff groaned.

"Be quick, father," urged Villa. "We must be on our way shortly."

Accoutring himself in his vestments, the priest stepped before the sheriff and the beauty with whom he had run away.

The short service was soon over.

"Now you are legally married," exclaimed Villa to his sister.

"Then everything is all right?" asked the sheriff who feared the short, heavy man before him.

"Yes."

"Good. We'll return to Las Nieves and celebrate."

"There's a little work to be done first," declared Villa. " 'Rico, get the spade attached to my saddle."

In amazement the others heard the orders and in amazement they watched the brother as he received the shovel from his friend.

His face, terrible to see, Villa turned on the sheriff.

"Take this shovel and dig a grave," he commanded.

As they heard the grim order, the others shrank back.

"What——" began the sheriff, only to be interrupted by his new-made brother-in-law.

"Don't ask questions but *dig*," cried Villa.

Fascinated, wondering what the brother intended to do, the others watched while the sheriff dug.

"That will do," exclaimed Villa, at last.

Quickly the sheriff straightened up.

At the same instant a gun barked and the man who had eloped with the beauty sunk down in the grave he had dug.

CHAPTER III.

VILLA ADMINISTERS THE OATH OF ALLEGIANCE.

Instinctively the others drew away from the man who had murdered his brother-in-law.

But Villa only laughed, picked up the shovel and threw in the earth upon the man he had killed.

"Father," said he when he had finished the task. "I want you to escort my sister safely back to the ranch at Las Nieves.

"Having put the sheriff out of the way, the State of Durango will not be a safe place for me."

Realizing protest would be vain, the priest agreed.

Part of the way, Villa and his companions accompanied them, then headed toward the Sierra Madre Mountains.

Francisco Villa, at the age of twenty, was a murderer, doomed by his act to a life of outlawry.

"You'd better come with me," he said to his friends. "You are accessories and can be shot as well as I."

Fearing to refuse the three cowboys agreed.

On the way they stopped at the Rondo ranch.

"Any money?" demanded Villa, as the owner stepped upon the porch to greet him.

"Yes."

"Get it."

"Never."

Again Villa's gun barked and the ranch owner dropped.

"Quick, inside and get the money," he cried.

In short order they opened the safe and found $2500.

"We'll burn the house to cover our work," Villa announced, as he stuffed the money into his shirt.

Reluctantly the others applied the torch; then went out to their horses and were riding away, when the Rondo cowboys dashed up, having been attracted by the shot.

As they saw the house in flames the punchers started for Villa and his men.

"Give them a shot," commanded the outlaw.

Again and again their guns barked, then the bandits

raced toward the Sierras and in due course reached a cave which Villa announced would be their head-quarters.

As he lay stretched out on the ground, the bandit leader determined to live up to his nickname, "The Tiger."

Visions of the rich ore wagons as they crawled along the trails from the mines to the railroad stations flashed into his mind.

At the same time, however, he realized that in order to be able to carry out any plans that came into his head he must have assistance—and he then and there determined to organize the band which has robbed, burned and murdered from one end of Mexico to the other.

Sitting up, he shouted: "Bepo, Dato, Enrico."

From the nooks they had selected, the three men came forth.

"Come here," Villa commanded, himself sitting up.

And when the trio had obeyed, he bade them seat themselves, rolled a cigarette and then studied the face of first one and then another.

At last he spoke:

"Before I outline my plans I want to remind you that I have each mother's son of you in my power.

"You were all with me when we robbed the safe of the Gringo's ranch. You were all with me when

we set fire to the storehouse. You each of you shot
at the Gringo cowpunchers.

"Whether those bullets killed any of them we don't
know.

"So I can hand every one of you over to the
Rurales for robbery, arson and murder—but I won't.

"If any one of you wants to leave after hearing
my plan, you can do so.

"But if any one does and he betrays me—or tries
to—he won't be alive after I meet him again. Just
get that in your heads and remember it."

As the heavy-lipped bandit warmed to his words,
he waved his hands and rolled his eyes, excitedly.

Terrified by his words, his companions watched his
every move, forgetting even to puff on their cigarettes
as they listened to what he said.

Suddenly he leaned forward.

"Do you want to leave, Dato?" he demanded, at the
same time pointing his finger at the man nearest him.

"N-no," faltered the half breed.

"Do you, Enrico?"

"No-o."

"Do you, Bepo?"

"No."

"Good. I'll make you rich. I'll make your names
so feared that you'll only have to tell who you are to
have women and Gringos hand over their money,

jewels and cattle to leave them alone.

"Peons can work for a peso a day if they want to, but I, Francisco Villa, will never take less than a thousand dollars, gold,—and I'll take it when I want it, and as often as I want it.

"Madre di Dios, but I'll live the life—money, women and pulque!

"Do you want to share them with me?"

Eyes big with greed, faces flushed with excitement, the three men chorused their eagerness to follow the bandit chieftain.

"Then take the oath of alligiance," exclaimed Villa. "And remember, each and every one of you must obey me in everything. Death will be the penalty for the slightest disobedience."

From his sash, Pancho drew a knife on whose blade dark spots showed that it had tasted blood.

"Swear on this," he said. "Dato, you first. Put your right hand on the blade and repeat what I say."

Fascinated, the half breed reached forth his hand, but as his fingers touched the blood spots, he drew it back.

"Don't be afraid—it's only Gringo blood," laughed Villa. "That's better. Now repeat:

" 'By the mother that bore me I swear to follow Francisco Villa wherever he may lead; to go wherever he tells me to go; to do whatever he tells me to do;

to give him all loot, money, jewels, women, cattle or horses I take and to accept willingly the portion he allots me; if I disobey him or betray him or any of his band, I hope my soul will rot in hell and my body become the food of snakes and tarantulas.'

"Now kiss the blade," commanded Villa as Dato, pale and trembling, finished repeating the terrible oath, which bound him, body and soul, to the bandit chieftain.

In turn, Bepo and Enrico swore their allegiance.

"Now go back where you were while I make my plans," ordered Pancho.

And rolling another cigarette, he stretched out on his back again, lazily blowing rings of smoke, while the three members of his band returned to their respective nooks in silence, too terrified by the awful oath they had sworn to talk among themselves.

CHAPTER IV.

THWARTED.

Toward sunset, the bandit chieftain, whose name was destined to become a horror throughout the civilized world, sat up.

"Bepo, get supper," he called. "Dato, you and 'Rico look to the horses and saddles. We ride to night."

As the trio went about Villa's commands, having recovered from the immediate terror of the oath they had taken, they talked with one another in low voices, wondering what their leader had in mind.

But Pancho, though he heard them, did not gratify their curiosity, devoting all his attention to cleaning the rifles and shooting irons they would take with them.

"Don't you want me to do that?" asked Bepo, waiting for the coffee to boil.

"No; when I attend to the guns myself, I know they are all right," the chieftain returned.

And his manner was so brusque that Bepo hurried back to his cook fire.

Not until they had finished eating and had lighted their cigarettes did the leader of the newly organized gang of bandits disclose his intention.

"It's lonesome in this cave," he declared, blowing out a cloud of smoke. "Any place is lonesome without a pretty face or two."

"But would any woman want to live way up in the Sierra Madre Mountains and in a cave at that?" inquired Dato.

"What difference does that make whether they want to or not?" the bandit leader demanded.

"Why, they wouldn't come if they didn't want to," returned the half breed.

"Oh, wouldn't they?" Pancho sneered.

"You just wait and see. Besides they won't have any say about it. We'll just get them and bring them here."

"Kidnap 'em, you mean?" asked 'Rico.

"If you want to call it that, yes."

"A-ah!" exclaimed Bepo, in deep satisfaction. "That is the good idea.

"There is a Gringo girl at the Los Rodas ranch that
I would like. I have asked her to marry me, but
she laugh and call me 'greaser.'

"I kissed her once and she boxed my ear. O-ow!"
And the bandit rubbed his ear as though it still tingled
from the blow.

"Good," chuckled Villa. "You shall have her.

"How about you, Dato? Any one in particular
you'd like?"

"No."

"And you, 'Rico?"

"I think the Senorita Dolores Gonzales, daughter
of the banker in Casas Grandes, is very beautiful."

"Then you shall have her."

"But she's Mexican," Dato exclaimed, in evident
surprise that the bandit chieftain should even think
of kidnapping one of his own nationality.

"That makes no difference," Pancho returned.
"When one of my band wants anything, he shall have
it—if I approve, or die in trying to get it.

"Myself, I like very much the looks of the wife of
the Americano who runs the Honora ranch."

Unconsciously his companions started as they heard
his words.

Grinning at the effect they produced, Pancho repeated:

"Yes, I like her looks very much.

"Come on it is a thirty-mile ride to the Honora ranch. We'll go there first. Then to Los Rodas, and tomorrow night we will get Dolores for you 'Rico."

As he concluded, Villa picked up his rifle, bade his men get theirs, and led the way to the plateau where the horses were hobbled.

"We'll have to get more horses," Pancho commented as he looked at the half dozen browsing.

"I intend to strike in all driections and it will mean hard riding. To do it, we must have plenty of fresh mounts to choose from."

The saddling and bridling took but a very short time and as the first shadows of evening fell across the trail, the four desperadoes rode down the mountain, the man whose black deeds have shocked the world in the lead.

Knowing almost every stone and bush in the region, Villa led his men at a stiff pace.

As though to further their dread purpose, the night came up cloudy and black.

Only the eyes of men accustomed to travel in the darkness could have detected the buildings of the Honora ranch when the bandits reached them, for it was close to midnight and no lights were burning in the home house or in the cow punchers' shack.

"Shall we ride to the shack while you go to the house?" Dato asked, in a whisper. "We three can stand off the Gringo punchers long enough for you to get the woman."

"There's no need of it," Pancho returned. "Harkness and the boys are out on the round-up. I found that out yesterday.

"Nobody home but the woman and the Chink cook.

"Now this is the way we'll do it. Dato, you'll go to the door and knock. When the Senora opens it, Bepo will grab her and swing her up onto my horse.

" 'Rico will stand by to deal with the Chink if he should try to make any trouble.

"All ready."

And the four men rode toward the home house.

Dismounting silently, Dato and Bepo approached the door.

With the butt of his six-shooter, Dato pounded on it.

Loudly the raps rang out in the midnight stillness, but though they listened intently, no sound of any one stirring within the house did the men bent on so foul a mission hear.

"Carramba! Can she be gone, too?" Villa growled. "Knock again, Dato."

Harder than before the half breed beat upon the door.

Came moments of silence, then suddenly a light shone from the windows in front of them.

Cursing furiously, Pancho hissed:

"Quick! get the horses over onto the other side in the dark."

Hurriedly Bepo and 'Rico obeyed.

In the light from the lamp, they could see the wife of the ranch owner moving toward the door.

"Be ready and quick, Bepo," Pancho breathed, setting himself to receive the prize he coveted.

But instead of opening the door, Mrs. Harkness called:

"Who's there?"

"A friend," answered the bandit chieftain.

"Friends don't come at this hour of the night," returned the ranch owner's wife. "Go away instantly or I'll shoot."

"But Mr. Harkness, he is hurt. He sent me for you," lied Villa.

"How does it happen he sent a Mexican when all our punchers are Americans? You can't fool me that way.

"If you don't go before I count five, I'll shoot."

"Beat in the door," roared the infuriated bandit chieftain.

As the butts of their rifles fell upon the door, the ranch owner's wife raised her pistol and fired.

Angered at the failure of his ruse, Pancho leaped from his horse, dashed to a window, kicked it in with his boot and sprang inside.

Her attention distracted from the door by the crashing of the window glass, Mrs. Harkness turned.

As her eyes fell upon the intruder, she staggered back.

"My God! Francisco Villa!" she gasped.

Then, clutching at her throat she stammered:

"W-what do you want?"

"You."

As he uttered the word, the man who had often shared their food with the cowboys of the Honora ranch and was, therefore, known to its mistress, leapt forward, swinging the barrel of his rifle so that it knocked the woman's pistol-hand aside.

"John! Help! John! John!" She shrieked in the effort to bring the Chinese cook to her assistance.

"No use," leered Pancho. "I have you now."

With a lightning movement, Villa seized the woman about the waist, swung about, shot out the light and dashed for the door which his men had opened.

Frantically his captive struggled but the bandit only laughed.

Suddenly a shot rang out.

Blood spurted over Pancho and he stopped.

"Madre di Dios! She's killed herself!" he cried.

A moment he stood as though abashed at the horror

his attack had wrought, then, with a volley of oaths, cast the body roughly to the ground, darted to his horse, leaped into the saddle and dashed away, followed by his horror-struck companions.

CHAPTER V.

THE KIDNAPPING.

Furious that his plan had failed, that it had ended so tragically, for the bandit chieftain was young in his career of blood and pillage and, therefore, less hardened than now, Villa rode at a wild pace.

And behind him, as best they could, his companions followed, too unnerved at the outcome of the kidnapping plot to talk to one another.

As the shock of the death of the owner of the Honora ranch lessened, Villa's anger rose.

Vain ever in his youth, it maddened him to think that a woman should prefer death to him. And as though to avenge himself, he rowelled his mount unmercifully with his spurs.

His first idea was to return to the cave in the Sierra Madres. But he feared the effect such a return, empty-handed, after he had vowed to bring back some pretty faces, might have upon his followers and those other Mexicans and Americans who would surely hear of the midnight raid and its sad ending, and with a savage oath, he shouted to his followers to ride up to him.

"The woman was a fool," he snarled. "I would have given her money and jewels. I'd have made her Queen of Bandits.

"But there are other women.

"How many are there at Los Rodas, Bepo?"

"Three. The Gringo girl and two English ones. But one, she is old. She is the mother."

"We'll take the two young ones."

And shaking out his mount, the terrible bandit, whose attempt to gratify his whim had resulted in the death of one noble woman, dashed over the arid plain.

Arrived at the ranch, Villa drew rein.

"Dato, you and 'Rico go to the shack and start shooting," he commanded. "Keep riding round and round, so that any punchers in it will think we are in force.

"Use both your six-shooters and your rifles. It will help fool the Gringos.

"Bepo, you and I will go to the house. The shots

from the shack will rouse those inside.

"When they appear, you seize your Gringo girl and I'll take the English one.

"If she resists, knock her unconscious.

"Go to it."

Little relishing the work, as they remembered the tragedy of the Honora ranch, the men moved off to perform their parts.

Dismounting, Pancho and Bepo went to the front door, then waited for their companions to begin firing.

Suddenly the silence of the night was shattered by the crash of guns and wild shouting as Dato and 'Rico dashed around the cowboys' shack.

"That's great! They'll think there are a lot of us," chuckled the bandit chieftain.

But the punchers of the Los Rodas ranch were to be reckoned with.

In a shortness of time that surprised even Villa himself, fire spat from the door and windows of the shack as the cowboys opened upon their attackers.

"Carramba! But we must get out of this," snarled Pancho. "Where are the women's quarters, do you know, Bepo?"

"They are on the other side, to the south."

"Then bring the horses round." And the bandit leader dashed round the corner of the house.

As he reached it, he saw to his delight that lamps were being hastily lighted.

"There won't be any danger of carrying off the old woman instead of the young one," he muttered to himself.

Springing upon the wide veranda Pancho crossed it, kicked in the window and leaped into the room, six-shooters in each hand.

"Not a sound!" he hissed as he beheld three women cowering before him. "You two young ones come here."

Outside the barking of the guns and the yelling of the bandits and the cowboys sounded awesomely.

But the women only cringed in the corner farthest from the wild-eyed man facing them.

"Don't make me use these things," he snarled, moving his revolvers back and forth. "You two young ones come here."

Just then Bepo entered through the broken window.

"Get them," commanded his chief.

As the American girl recognized the man whose ears she had boxed, she cried out in fright.

But Bepo only grinned.

Quickly he seized her about the waist.

With all her strength, the girl raised her two hands and brought them down full upon the bandit's nose.

Like a fountain the blood spurted.

Crazed by the pain, Bepo nevertheless remembered his master's instructions and raising his six-shooter, he brought it down upon the girl's head, dropping her to the floor.

"I've got you now," he gloated. "You'll not strike me again." And stooping over, he picked up the American girl in his arms and carried her from the room.

When they realized the purpose of the attack, the English women dropped to their knees and raised their hands in prayer.

"Your God won't help you now," mocked the bandit chieftain. "You'd better worship a man who has two hands and can use them."

And with a hideous laugh, Pancho seized the girl's wrists and jerked her to her feet.

"Follow me!" he hissed, dragging her after him as he started for the window.

"Wait! Stop!" wailed the elder English woman. "Take my jewels, take the money, the silver I have, but spare me my daughter."

And in her appeal the woman got to her feet and clutched the bandit's coat.

In answer, he turned, kicked her full in the face, grabbed his captive in his arms and dashed out into the night.

As the terrible outlaw stepped upon the veranda,

he met the superintendent of the ranch, six-shooter in hand.

"Drop that girl!" thundered the Englishman, at the same time pulling the trigger of his revolver which he aimed at the maurauler's legs lest he injure the woman in his arms.

It was a desperate moment for the bandit chieftain.

But no shot rang from the gun.

The luck which has led his followers and the people of Mexico to believe he has a charmed life came to Villa's aid.

The cylinder of the superintendent's revolver was empty.

Cursing the fact, the Englishman shoved a couple of cartridges into the gun and fired.

But by the time the shot rang out, Pancho was on his horse, his captive in front of him.

With a fiendish laugh, he waved his hand at the superintendent and leaped his mount forward.

"Come on! We've got them!" yelled Villa to Dato and 'Rico as he rounded the corner of the house.

And as his men joined him, he whirled his mount and raced in the direction of his cave in the mountains, while the curses and shots of the cowboys reached after him.

CHAPTER VI.

VILLA OUTWITS HIS PURSUERS.

But the brutal bandit was not to get to his cave in the fastnesses of the Sierra Madres unmolested.

Even as the desperate band rode away, the Englishman rushed to the cow punchers' shack.

"Into the saddles, my lads," he shouted. "The greasers have carried off Miss Wales and Betty Moore."

"They'll not get far with Betty!" growled one of the boys whose love for the girl had made him the butt for the jokes of all his fellow-punchers. "I'll cut the heart out of the dirty hound who's dared to lay hand on her!"

"We'll help!" chorused others of the ranch crew who heard the vow.

For Betty, who served as maid and companion to the English girl, was a general favorite.

But even had she not been, it would have made no difference, for she was an American girl and the man who had dared to carry her off was a greaser.

Rushing to the corral, the punchers caught and saddled their horses.

"I'll join you directly," said Hastings, the superintendent. "I must tell Mrs. Wales we are going after her daughter and Betty."

But when he entered the room, Hastings stopped, abashed.

Huddled in a heap lay Mrs. Wales, blood oozing from the cuts in her face made by Villa's boot.

"The dirty robbers!" he snarled, as he raised the elderly woman and carried her to her bed.

But the superintendent, realizing that time was precious, made her as comfortable as he could, then rejoined the impatient punchers, three of whom he detailed to remain behind to guard the ranch and to assist Mrs. Wales.

"They've a good mile start of us," lamented Betty's lover, Shorty, as Hastings gave the word to ride.

"But their horses are fagged, while ours are fresh," returned the Englishman. "Besides two of them are double-loaded.

"Come on, lads, we can catch up with them in half an hour."

Riding as only cowboys can, the avenging troop raced over the prairie.

As the pounding of the hoofs reached Villa's ears, he cursed.

"They'll get us," moaned 'Rico.

"They may get you but not me," returned the bandit chieftain. "No Gringo, no Englishman, not even a Mexican can kill Francisco Villa.

"Didn't you see how the Englishman shot at me, point blank?"

"But his gun wasn't loaded," exclaimed Bepo.

"I don't care what the cause, he didn't get me. That's Villa luck. My life is charmed. Remember that and tell every one you see about it."

All the while, though they were riding as hard as they could, the bandits quickly realized that the pursuers were gaining on them.

In a trice, Pancho made his plans, for he was well aware that his prestige would suffer if his kidnapping the two girls was frustrated.

" 'Rico, ride close. Take the girl and go for the cave as though all the fiends of hell were at your heels.

"Bepo, you go with him.

"Dato, you and I will show these Gringos that it isn't safe to trail Pancho Villa! When you hear us fire, 'Rico, one of you shoot, too."

As the commands were finished, the horses descended into a deep roll in the plains.

"We'll ride over here to the right," said the bandit chieftain. "When the Gringos come over the edge, use your rifle."

At such a pace were the cowboys riding that Villa and his man had barely reached their positions when the punchers dashed over the top of the roll.

"Now!" whispered Pancho. And his rifle crashed even as he spoke.

An instant later, Dato's rang out.

And from the cowboys, a yell of pain told them that one of their bullets had found human flesh.

Surprised that the shots came from the right, when they thought the kidnappers were directly ahead of them, the pursuers lost no time in answering the shots, yelling and whooping as they raced in the direction whence they came.

As they did, a shot sounded to the left, for 'Rico had obeyed his master.

"They've split up!" cried Hastings. "I wonder which party the girls are with."

"The one to the left," declared Shorty. "It's

farther away and that proves these other greasers are trying to draw us off so those with Betty can make their getaway."

"Jove! I believe you're right," exclaimed the Englishman.

"Sure he is!" chorused several of the others.

"Then we'll follow in that direction," Hastings announced, while Shorty and some of the others cursed the delay the diversion in the gully had caused.

When Villa realized that his attempt to draw off the pursuers had been successful only for the moment, he cursed frightfully.

"We must join the others," he said to Dato. "We'll ride round the punchers' flank."

The task was not easy, for the bandits' horses were fast tiring, but by dint of desperate rowelling they managed to urge their mounts to greater speed and succeeded.

But as they rejoined Bepo and 'Rico, Pancho realized that the effort had taken the last power of their ponies.

"They'll get us," wailed Dato.

"Cut that!" Pancho snarled.

"But my pony is slackening up and the others will soon, carrying double."

His master, however, made him no answer.

Already Villa was aware of the facts Dato stated.

But his resourcefulness which has so bothered those who have tried to capture or trap the notorious cut-throat, came to his rescue.

Sliding from his saddle, Pancho wet his finger, held it in the air only long enough to learn that the wind came from the direction he was going, then stooped, lighted a match and set the dry prairie grass on fire.

Bidding Dato start fires to the left, Pancho dashed along, applying the match every few rods until in a few minutes there was a long wall of fire rushing upon the pursuing cowboys.

As the men from Los Rodas grasped what the terrible bandit had done, they shrieked and cursed, firing wildly in their fury, out of range though they were.

And in answer, Pancho and his men shouted derisively.

CHAPTER VII.

SHORTY TAKES UP THE TRAIL.

As they saw the wall of fire bearing down upon them by leaps and bounds, the cow punchers realized that if they were to escape with their lives, they must ride like the wind.

Shorty and Hastings alone stood out against returning.

"We can ride through," protested Betty's lover.

"You can't ride through hell on a horse of flesh and blood," declared Big Mike, the foreman. "And if anything looks like my idea of hell, it's that leaping, dancing stretch of flame."

"But it will be deserting the girls to their fate at the hands of those bally robbers," the superintendent exclaimed.

"Well, you'd be burned up if you tried to go to them, so I don't see how they'd be any better off," declared Big Mike. "If we can outride this blaze we'll be able to start back after them when it dies out."

The futility of trying to ride through the fire at last struck Shorty and he headed with his companions toward Los Rodas, but as he rode, he promised himself that he would go after Betty as soon as he could and not return till he found her.

Confident of their safety, the bandits pulled their wearied mounts down to a walk until they were rested, after which they made the cave without adventure.

During the day, word ran from ranch to ranch of the death of Mrs. Harkness of the Honora ranch, and the kidnapping of Betty and Miss Wales.

And everywhere there was a peon ran the whisper that it was Francisco Villa who led the raids.

On all sides, the malcontents and criminals pricked up their ears.

Here was a man who had dared to raid the ranches of two of the most wealthy and powerful men in the State of Durango.

Everywhere, among Rurales and peons, it was realized that Francisco Villa had defied the authorities of law and order as they existed in Mexico, and that he had, of his own free will and because of the impulsiveness of his nature, placed himself as a warrior against the then constituted authorities.

The lawless element rejoiced. Under such a leader, whose resourcefulness was shown in the way he had blocked his pursuers by firing the prairie, they realized that pickings would be fat.

Accordingly many a man saddled his pony and set out to join the man, the man who had shot a sheriff and followed the act on the next night by stealing $2500, and within a few days by kidnapping the daughter of a powerful land owner.

But they soon found it was one thing to wish to join the bandit and quite another to know where to find him.

The most crafty inquiries failed to develop his whereabouts. '

Beyond the fact that he was known to have been riding toward the Sierra Madre Mountains with the girls he had captured, nothing definite could be ascertained—and there were countless fastnesses in the mountain range where the most daring outlaw Mexico had ever known might hide.

But the criminals who wished to proclaim him as their leader were not the only ones who sought him.

As the reports of his raids, with the death of Mrs. Harkness, and the owner of the Ronda ranch, and the kidnapping of the women from Los Rodas were received by the authorities, the commander of the

Rurales in the State of Durango grew furious.

Ordering the captain before him, General Hoda exclaimed:

"You must capture this murderer. Take fifty men and go after him. If they are not enough, call on me for more. Villa must be rounded up."

Aware, from the very daring the bandit had displayed in executing his raids, that he had no easy task before him, Don Sebastian Gomez, captain of the Rurales, picked fifty of his best men from his command and set out upon his mission—a mission that engaged not only him but the Rurales of other States than Durango for fifteen years, at the end of which they saw the man they had hunted elevated to a military command in the forces of the revolutionary leader, Francisco Madero, and later win his way among the masses of peons and military men alike to the rank of a national hero.

But while the authorities were moving to compass his capture, Villa was planning new depredations.

The results of his raid, considered successes from his point of view, made him eager to attempt greater crimes.

"They have nicknamed me 'The Tiger,' " he said to his three companions, "so I am going to let them feel my teeth.

"The first thing we need is more men. In order

to carry out my plans, we four are not enough.

"I have no doubt the Rurales are already on my trail. If we meet them, we must be able to overpower them. They do not travel in twos or threes when hunting a man like me.

"Therefore we must increase our numbers. Do any of you know a man who can be trusted?"

Thus appealed to, his companions quickly named a score or more of peons whom they knew would be only to glad to join such a leader.

"We don't want as many as that," Villa returned. "It is easier to strike and get away with nine or ten men than it is with twenty.

"When we are rested we will set out and talk with your friends."

Before this time came, however, the bandits were made aware that the retreat in which they thought they would be safe was not known to themselves alone.

Thinking only of rescuing the girl of his heart from the hated greaser bandits, no sooner had Shorty returned to Los Rodas after escaping from the prairie fire than he determined to take up the pursuit.

"I know this Francisco Villa," he told the other punchers. "That is, I mean I've seen him. He's a half breed and so in love with himself that there is nothing he would not think he can do.

"But he's a greaser—and therefore a bluffer.

"I'm going to get him. Anybody want to go with me?"

"You don't even know where he is," protested Big Mike. "What's the use of wasting your time and probably losing your life in hunting him? The Rurales are already on his trail. Better leave it to them."

"But Betty, think of her," exclaimed the cowboy.

"I don't like to," answered the foreman.

"Nor I—and that's why I'm going to rescue her," Shorty returned, and went away from the shack in front of which he and the other punchers had been talking to the corral.

Quickly selecting his pony, the cowboy lover saddled and bridled him.

"Anybody going with me?" he asked as he rode from the corral.

Uneasily the other punchers shifted from one foot to another.

"Can't spare 'em," Big Mike finally said. "Of course, with you it's different. You've been sweet on Betty ever since you came to Los Rodas. If you want to go after her, I won't stop you—and I don't blame you. But I can't spare the other boys, with the round-up coming on."

For several moments, Shorty looked at the men with whom he had shared the trials and joys of the ranch life.

None of them, however, volunteered to accompany him.

With a snort of disgust, Shorty gathered up his reins.

"You're a fine bunch of huskies," he exclaimed. "Bad as I hate the greasers, I think I'd rather have them for friends than you."

And digging his spurs into his pony, the cowboy galloped from Los Rodas.

CHAPTER VIII.

THE TORTURE.

Confident that the kidnappers of his sweetheart had sought safety in the mountains, Shorty rode straight for them.

It was not long before he met some of the Mexicans who were also seeking the daring bandit, but from entirely different motives.

Coming upon a group sitting about a camp-fire just at sunset, the cowboy drew rein.

"What do you want?" demanded one of the Mexicans, while they all eyed him with suspicion.

"I'm looking for a friend," Shorty lied.

"Well, he's not with us," snapped the man.

"So I see," the cowboy returned. "I'm sorry. I've ridden hard. Are you Rurales?"

The question was needless, for the men did not wear the uniform of the mounted police of Mexico and Shorty knew it, but he thought he might gain their confidence by seeming ignorant.

His question was greeted with roars of laughter.

"Well, hardly!" said the spokesman at last.

"I'm glad," said Shorty, dismounting.

Unconcernedly he seated himself at the fire, and in a little while he had declared himself an outlaw who, attracted by the daring of Villa's raids, was determined to join him.

"That's what we're going to do," said one of the Mexicans.

"Know where he is?" Shorty asked, with all the disinterestedness he could assume.

"In the Sierras, of course. And I think he's in a cave near the head of the great pass," declared one of the men.

This statement brought on a discussion among the others, each of whom held a different opinion as to the bandit's whereabouts.

Closely Shorty listened to all they said, fixing in his mind the various retreats they mentioned.

When at last the Mexicans made ready to sleep, the cowboy got up.

"Where going?" called one of them.

"To join Pancho."

"Why not wait till morning?"

"Because the sooner I find him, the safer I shall feel," and saddling, Shorty rode away.

Early the next morning he was riding up the trail which led to the cave by the great pass when a bullet whistled close to his head.

Dato, who had arisen early, had discovered the lone horseman advancing toward his master's retreat and deemed it wise to find out who he was.

Drawing rein, as the bullet sped past his head, Shorty looked about him.

"Hands up!" shouted Dato, appearing from behind a rock at the head of the trail.

Quickly the cowboy obeyed.

"What do you want?" demanded the bandit.

"To find Pancho, The Tiger."

"Why?"

"Because I want to ride with him."

The sound of the shot had aroused the bandit leader and as Dato was questioning the cowboy, he appeared upon the scene.

"What is it?" Villa inquired.

"This Gringo wants to join The Tiger," Dato replied.

"Why?" asked Villa, coming close to Shorty.

"Because you're a man after my own heart," the cowboy replied.

The praise flattered The Tiger and he smiled.

"Come up to the cave," he exclaimed, and waiting till Shorty was in front of him, he followed.

Elated at his success in locating the bandit who had carried off his sweetheart, Shorty was busy mapping out a story that would assure Villa of his willingness to ride with him when they reached the cave.

Bidding the cowboy dismount, Pancho squatted and signed Shorty to do so.

Keenly Villa questioned him, and the cowboy was apparently giving satisfactory answers when a woman's shriek broke on their ears.

Instantly Shorty recognized Betty's voice and the thought that she was being subjected to treatment that caused her to cry out filled him with fury.

"What's that?" he demanded, springing to his feet.

"Nothing but Bepo making love to the Americano we brought from Los Rodas," returned Villa.

"But why should she cry out?" pursued the cowboy.

In answer the bandit chieftain merely shrugged his shoulders.

"But do you allow your men to treat their captives so?" demanded Shorty.

Again The Tiger shrugged his shoulders, adding, "It is none of our business, anyhow."

Wild at the thoughts which surged through his mind, the cowboy was on the point of trying to draw his gun, when more shrieks came from the cave.

Turning, both men saw a woman dart from its entrance closely pursued by a Mexican with a whip.

It was Betty.

Straight toward the two by the rock she came.

Suddenly she recognized the cowboy.

"Oh, Shorty, save me! Save me!" she wailed, rushing to him.

Ere the cowboy could move, The Tiger was on his feet, a six-shooter in each hand.

His face was distorted with fury and his eyes blazed.

"So you are a friend of the Gringo girl? You would trick The Tiger, would you?" hissed Villa, with a volley of oaths. "It was a sorry day for you when you came to his lair.

"Hand me your gun."

By this time Bepo had his hands upon Betty.

Turning, she struck him full in the face.

Cursing frightfully, the Mexican brought the butt of his whip down on her head, felling her.

Heedless of consequences, Shorty leaped at Bepo, arm upraised.

Instantly a pistol spoke and the cowboy's arm dropped.

"Take the girl back to the cave, Bepo," Pancho commanded. "Send 'Rico and Dato to me."

Stooping Bepo touched Betty.

"Don't take me back—kill me first!" she pleaded.

"Quick, take her away," thundered Villa, then called, "'Rico! Dato!"

Struggling every inch of the way, the girl was dragged into the cave by Bepo, while Shorty, held motionless by The Tiger's six-shooter, was compelled to look on.

Quickly the two men he had summoned joined the bandit.

"Take this man down to the camp-fire," he commanded. "I'll be there directly."

And as the greasers led Shorty away Villa entered the cave.

In a moment he reappeared, carrying an iron bar.

Going to the camp-fire, he thrust it into the coals.

"Take off his shirt," snapped The Tiger, pointing to the cowboy.

This done, the four waited while Villa tested the heat of the iron bar.

At last it satisfied him.

Raising it, he laid it full length across Shorty's back.

Again and again, he repeated the terrible torture, till at last the cowboy, unable longer to bear the awful pain, swooned and fell to the ground.

"Now saddle up," ordered the Tiger. "We'll take this Gringo back to Los Rodas.

"Perhaps it will serve as a warning to other white-faced Americano or English pigs that they cannot capture Francisco Villa single-handed, and that it is dangerous to come to his retreat."

CHAPTER IX.

THE CATTLE DRIVE.

It was dark when The Tiger with his companions and the man he had tortured so fiendishly arrived at the Los Rodas ranch.

Lights in the cow punchers' shack told the bandit leader that the men were at home. And when he got closer to the ranch, the odor told him that the cattle were also there.

With this discovery, his spirits rose.

Calling his three companions to him, he exclaimed:

"They say lightning never strikes twice in the same place—but The Tiger does.

"The Los Rodas cattle have been driven in from the round-up. There are no fatter or better blooded cattle in Durango. They will bring a fancy price.

"We need the money more than the white-faced pig,
Wales.

"When we leave Los Rodas, we will take the cattle
with us."

The boldness of the plan amazed the three other
bandits.

"But the punchers will all be home if the cattle are.
We can never get away with them. Better wait till
they are out on the range again," cautioned 'Rico.

"I have said we would take the cattle with us," returned Villa, "That ends it."

"But the punchers," repeated 'Rico.

"They were here when we carried off the women.
They are not to be feared," snapped the leader, and
again rode ahead.

He was, however, too awake to the danger of his
purpose not to move with extreme caution, and when
they were within a few hundred yards of the ranch
house he halted.

Swinging the tightly bound and gagged cowboy from
the horse on which he had ridden, to his own, Villa
bade his companions await him.

"If you hear any shooting, ride it, he whispered.
"Otherwise stay here till I return."

With utmost caution the bandit chieftain advanced
upon the ranch house.

When a hundred feet away, he halted.

Shouts and laughter from the shack told him that the punchers were gambling, and he smiled, realizing that their attention was riveted upon their game.

In the home house there was neither sound nor light.

Dismounting, Pancho lifted his victim to the ground, where he securely bound his feet.

Then, picking him up, he made his way stealthily, with all the craft of the tiger whose name he had been given; he approached the veranda.

Mounting it, he placed Shorty's body in front of the door in such a way that any one coming out would trip over it.

Turning, he shook his fist at the ranch house, went back to his horse, mounted and quickly rejoined the men who were anxiously awaiting him.

"Now for the cattle," he whispered.

"You men know how to ride them. Dato and I will take the rear, Bepo, you ride the right flank, 'Rico the left.

"We'll drive them through the Arondo pass to market.

"If the punchers attack us, I will stand them off and you, Dato, will ride the rear alone.

"Should I be obliged to separate from you, drive hard. Don't be afraid of running off any flesh. We

can rest the cattle in the Hontos plateau before taking
them to market.

"Ready."

But when the bandits came upon the cattle, they
were disappointed.

Instead of the big herd they had hoped to find,
there were not more than a hundred.

"A stray bunch picked up," snarled Villa. "However, the fewer the easier to drive and even a hundred
of the Los Rodas cattle are worth money.

"When you and 'Rico have taken your positions,
whistle Bepo. Now go."

Ears alert for any sound of discovery from ranch
house or shack, The Tiger and Dato awaited the
signal.

All at once, a light flashed from the door of the
ranch house, followed by a shout as the body of
Shorty was found.

The cry reached the ears of the punchers in the
shack, as well as the bandits, and they streamed from
the door.

"They've brought Shorty back," shouted the superintendent of the ranch, who had discovered the bound
and gagged cowboy.

Instantly the punchers ran to the veranda.

"The fiends!" snarled Big Mike, as they beheld the
terrible wounds on Shorty's back. "Round-up or no

round-up, we'll go after The Tiger. The nerve of
him bringing Shorty to us again."

In the momentary lull which followed the foreman's
words there rang out two whistles, the signals from
'Rico and Bepo to their master.

"What's that?" chorused several of the cow
punchers.

And their answer came in the snorting and lowing
of the cattle as the bandits jumped them into running.

"The dirty greasers are after the two-year olds,"
Big Mike cried. "Quick! every mother's son of you.
Get your guns and horses. By heaven, this is too
much."

Away raced the cowboys to prepare themselves, and
to their ears came the thunder of hoofs as the cattle
were rushed along.

In remarkably short time, the boys of Los Rodas
were in pursuit.

"I see them! I see the dirty devils," shouted one
of the punchers, and instantly he opened fire.

Quickly the others followed suit, and a veritable
rain of lead was poured at the bobbing figures of the
horsemen with the cattle.

Though the discovery and pursuit had come sooner
than he expected, Villa was, as ever, equal to the
emergency.

"You go through with the cattle, Dato," he commanded.

"I will draw the punchers off.

"By riding hard, you should make the mountains by sunrise.

"I'll meet you at the Hondas plateau some time tomorrow."

As he spoke, The Tiger whirled his horse, stood up in his stirrups and rode at right angles to the course the cattle were being driven.

Quickly there came a lull in the shots from the punchers as they reloaded their rifles.

Taking advantage of it, Villa again whirled his horse and rode straight at his pursuers.

"Come on, you pale-faced pigs!" he yelled. "Come on if you think you can catch The Tiger.

"But you never will. It makes no difference if you are one or a hundred. I, Francisco Villa, am your match."

And as he ended his maddening taunt, the bandit emptied the magazine of his rifle into the ranks of his pursuers.

Crazed by his words, the cow punchers whirled in his direction, yelling and shouting as they gave chase.

"Never mind the cattle, get that Mexican devil!" shouted Big Mike. "We can pick up the cattle after we get him."

"Yes, after you get him," The Tiger shouted back in derision, "But if you wait till then, the cattle will be dead."

Despite his bravado, the bandit leader was no fool, however, and, realizing that a chance bullet might find him, he clapped his spurs to his mount and raced in the direction away from the cattle, the cowboys in full cry after him, their bullets whistling on all sides of him.

CHAPTER X.

VILLA OUTWITS HIS PURSUERS.

Fortunately for the bandit chieftain, the horse on which he was mounted was a thoroughbred, and good though the ponies were on which the pursuing cowboys rode, The Tiger was soon carried out of range of their rifles.

As they realized the fact that their bullets were falling short of the man they so desired to catch, the cow punchers ceased firing and devoted all their attention to getting every possible ounce of speed out of their pintoes.

Aware that while he might keep a safe distance ahead of the men from Los Rodas that he could not hope to shake them off, Villa determined to try a change in direction.

The night had been starlit, with occasional clouds,

but the resultant darkness had been a sufficient cloak for the daring raid of the bandits.

But just as Villa turned his course, the moon came out.

That by its light they discovered the whereabouts of the outlaw was evident by the shouts which rose from the throats of the cowboys, some of whom, in their delight at having their quarry in sight, blazed away with their rifles despite the fact that the act was but a waste of ammunition.

Recking little that he had been located, so confident was he in the ability of his mount to outrun the cow horses, Villa raced over the prairie which now glistened like a vast silver lake on all sides of him.

And as he rode, he thought as to what part of the mountains he should enter.

As his mind was thus engrossed, he did not notice the dark specks which appeared on his right.

Nearer and nearer came the lone horseman and this second group of riders together, and still the bandit chieftain did not notice it.

Suddenly a shot rang out—and The Tiger's pointed sombrero sailed from his head.

"Madre di Dios! but I am glad my head is no taller!" he exclaimed. "That hat will cost somebody a lot of money. I wonder who this new crowd are."

The shot, however, told him that they were enemies,

thus making his situation more difficult, for the new-comers were in such a position that, if their horses were mettlesome, they could ride in between him and the mountains, and cut him off from his retreat.

The shot also told the pursuing cowboys that they were to have aid in rounding up The Tiger, and they shouted and yelled in their delight.

"Who do you suppose they are?" asked one of the punchers.

"Rurales," returned Big Mike.

"But Mexicans don't hunt at night, they prefer to sleep," declared another.

"They'll hunt night and day for Villa," said the foreman. "Mr. Wales and Bob Harkness are personal friends of President Diaz and they've made the wires hum to Mexico City since the cutthroat raided their ranches.

"Just the same, I bet the Rurales never get him," declared the first cow puncher.

"It looks as though we had him now," returned Big Mike. "Hello, what's The Tiger up to?"

The foreman's words drew the attention of the cow-boys again to the lone horseman.

Villa had realized that with two bands of pursuers right at his heels, he could never hope to reach any of the passes by which alone the Sierra Madre Moun-tains could be travelled. And with this realization, he had determined upon a desperate course.

Only his sublime belief in himself could have achieved it. But no sooner had it come into his mind than he took it.

Taking advantage of a roll in the plains, he rode with might and main along it, then turned again and headed straight for Los Rodas.

His detour was so wide that as he rose again from the roll, his figure would have been scarcely discernible had his pursuers been looking for him. But they were ignorant of his latest move and, though he saw them riding in the direction he had once been taking, they did not see him.

Easing his thoroughbred when he knew that he was no longer being chased by the cow punchers and Rurales, the fearless bandit rode leisurely toward Los Rodas.

The silence of the tomb was upon the ranch when he arrived.

Chuckling at the ease with which he had thrown off pursuit, Villa proceeded to carry out the plan he had formulated during his long ride.

Dismounting, he went to the wood shed and gathered a big bunch of dried chips.

These he placed about the ranch house, then returned to the shed, where he gathered more chips, which he piled about the cowboys' shack.

This done, he stealthily entered the cooking room and found the kerosene can.

With it he soaked the various heaps of chips.

When all had been saturated with the oil, he returned to the home house and, little caring whether any one was within, applied matches to each pile of the inflammable material.

As though inspired by the same hatred which he bore for pale-faced pigs, the flames leaped up and attacked the shingles with which the ranch house was covered.

Pausing only to see that each pile of chips was doing the duty he had assigned it, The Tiger hurried to fire the shack.

As the flames leaped high in the air he laughed.

"They'll learn better than to try to hunt Francisco Villa to his lair," he exclaimed aloud. "I only hope the men who were trailing me see the blaze."

For many minutes, the daring bandit watched the buildings burn, but he was ever mindful of the cattle which had been driven away, and at last he decided to join his companions.

His thoroughbred, however, was sorely spent by the hard rides to which the outlaw had subjected him, and as Pancho looked him over, he shook his head.

"You're not good for many more miles tonight, boy," he said. Then suddenly he remembered that in the corral was the best-blooded stallion in the State of Durango.

"Fair exchange is no robbery," he said to himself. "I may be many things but I am not a horse thief."

But his mind was made up to take the stallion, nevertheless.

So leading his own mount, he made his way to the horse corral.

Arrived there it was but the work of a few minutes to unsaddle his thoroughbred and saddle the stallion.

The latter task, however, to a man less proficient in the handling of horses would have been an impossible task.

But Villa knew horse flesh almost as well as he did his own soul, and despite the stallion's cavortings, he swung into the saddle and rode from the corral.

As he emerged, he saw the aged woman he had kicked in the face when he had kidnapped Betty and Miss Wales rushing about the burning buildings, wringing her hands.

"When the white-faced pigs get back, tell them they had better stay home instead of trying to ride down The Tiger," he shouted as he galloped by her.

At the sound of the voice, Miss Wales turned and caught sight of the bandit.

"God will punish you!" she cried.

But Villa only laughed.

"You'd better place your faith in men who can do things," he shouted back and rode out onto the plains.

CHAPTER XI.

The Tiger Recruits His Band.

Caring naught for the ruin he had wrought, the bandit galloped over the prairie revelling in the power of the horse under him.

Hard he rode over the course his men had driven the cattle and a little after sunrise he caught up with them.

Pausing only long enough to allow the cattle a breathing spell, Villa assisted in their drive to the Hontas plateau.

"We'll let them graze here," he announced as they reached the broad expanse in the Sierras. "They'll be safe for a day, at least.

"What I want is more men."

His companions, realizing as never before the desperateness of the life upon which they had entered, only suggested the names of two or three peons who had earned the title of "bad men," instead of the many they had mentioned when asked before.

"Lead me to them," commanded the bandit. "The Rurales will be upon us in force before many days—and I would rather be captured or shot by one of the white-faced Americano pigs than by one of them.

"We'll eat and then we'll look over your friends."

During the meal The Tiger related the story of his escape from the two bands of pursuers and the burning of the Los Rodas ranch buildings.

"That means the Los Rodas cow punchers will hang to our trail till we either get them or they get us," declared Dato.

"Let them," returned his master. "The more the merrier. I'm going to make the land owners and rich men in Mexico sit up and take notice."

Suddenly 'Rico sat erect.

"I wonder if that Shorty will lead the Los Rodas boys to the cave where the women are?" he exclaimed.

"I never thought of that," Villa returned. "You and Bepo had better ride over there. Take the girls and bring them to the bear cave.

"Dato and I can pick up enough men."

Accordingly when the bandits set out, the two

former headed for the cave by the great pass, while the two latter rode toward Casas Grandes.

As they neared the foot of the mountains, Villa drew rein.

"Some one coming," he whispered to Dato, and jumped his stallion into the brush beside the trail, where his man followed.

With guns ready for instant use the two bandits waited.

Nearer and nearer came the ring of hoof beats on the rocky trail, and soon six riders appeared.

"They're not Rurales," whispered Dato, "and they're not Gringos. What do you suppose they want?"

"We'll find out," returned his chief, and then without showing himself, he shouted:

"Halt—and hands up!"

Startled at the suddenness of this command the riders drew rein, looking about to discover the utterer.

But none of them raised their hands.

Suddenly six shots rang out—and six hats sailed from the heads of their wearers.

And almost before the last pointed sombrero had dropped, Villa yelled:

"I said 'hands up'—so be lively!"

Terrified both by the command and the warning shots, five of the horsemen thrust their hands over their heads.

"Come you, up with yours, too," called The Tiger to the sixth rider.

But instead of complying, the fellow whipped out his gun.

Ere he could use it, however, a bullet jerked it from his hand.

"Now put them up," said the bandit chieftain, and the man slowly obeyed.

"What do you want and who are you?" demanded Villa.

"We're looking for The Tiger," returned the man at the head of the line.

"Why?"

"Because we want to join him."

"Is that so?"

"Yes, I swear it by the head of my mother."

In turn Villa asked each of the other five the same questions and received the same answers.

"Well, here's The Tiger," cried Villa, leaping his stallion into the trail.

At the sight of the man who had wrought such havoc in so short a time, the strange horsemen gasped with amazement.

Enjoying the effect of his startling appearance, The Tiger looked the men over carefully.

"There'll only one of you do," he finally declared,

"and he's the one who drew his gun instead of putting up his hands.

"The Tiger has no use for men in his band who will quietly put themselves at the mercy of an unseen person.

"Suppose you were in my band and I had been a Rurale.

"A fine story it would have been for the curs to brag about in their barracks."

Deeply chagrined by the terrible bandit's words, the five sought to offer all sorts of excuses.

Villa only laughed at them, however.

"You can't lie any better than you can take care of yourselves, he finally sneered.

"Be off with you if you want to go with whole skins.

"Stranger," and he nodded to the rider whose actions had won his approval, "Come here."

"What's your name?" he asked as the man obeyed.

"Tomasso."

"Tomasso what?"

"Never mind."

The defiance brought a hot flush to The Tiger's cheeks.

"You refuse to answer?" he thundered.

"It's none of your business. I'm known as Tomasso, that's good enough."

Quickly Villa raised his six-shooter.

But the horseman looked him straight in the eye, never flinching.

Finally The Tiger lowered his weapon.

"You have the nerve I want in my men," he said. "You can ride with me if you will take the oath of allegiance.

"Are you willing?"

"Sure."

"All right. Repeat it after me."

But before he spoke the words of the terrible oath, Villa turned on the other horsemen.

"I told you to begone. So go while you have the chance." And again he raised his shooting irons.

"Then we'll hunt you with the Rural—" began one of them.

But before he had finished his threat the bandit chieftain's guns barked and the man tumbled from his horse.

"The rest of you had better get a move on," he exclaimed.

And as the men clapped spurs to their mounts and galloped down the trail The Tiger laughed.

"They're fainter-hearted than any white-faced pigs," he sneered. "Now for the oath, Tomasso."

"Fire away, I'm waiting," returned the new recruit to the band that was to terrorize Mexico.

Quickly the bandit chieftain spoke it and as quickly Tomasso repeated it.

"Now we'll go on our way," Villa declared, and started down the trail.

One after another, The Tiger added four men suggested by Dato, to his band, Felix, Baptista, Pulque and Rambo.

When the last of the quartette had taken the oath, Villa exclaimed:

"Now we are nine. That's enough.

"We'll go to the bear cave, get 'Rico and Bepo, and then see if we can't stir up some excitement."

CHAPTER XII.

THE TIGER IS TRACKED TO HIS LAIR.

Elated by the success of his raids, Villa gave no thought to the men who were hunting him once he and his recruits had gained the mountains again.

But the punchers from Los Rodas and the Rurales were diligently searching the mountains for him.

The trail of the cattle was, of course, easy for them to find, and they followed it to the Hontas plateau.

Glad though Big Mike was to recover the herd, which he sent back to the ranch under the care of three of his punchers, he and the others were greatly disappointed not to find the bandits with them.

"Wonder if they are on another raid?" suggested Don Sebastian, the captain of the Rurales.

"More likely they have gone to the cave by the great pass that Shorty told us about, for the girls," declared one of the cowboys.

"That's so," acquiesced the foreman. "We'll go there, too. If the dirty devils aren't there, we may be able to rescue Betty and Miss Wales; if they are there, we'll get The Tiger as well as the girls."

This plan met with the approval of the captain of the Rurales, and in quick order the troop started for the cave.

On their way, they met the four horsemen whom Villa had refused to enlist in his band.

Eagerly they related their treatment at the hands of the terrible bandit and begged to be allowed to join the avengers and hunt him.

Their services were accepted and the cavalcade changed its course to the trail to Bear Cave.

Little dreaming that his hiding place would be so quickly found, The Tiger decided to take a few days' rest before executing any more raids.

And this decision proved costly.

The bandit chieftain and his men were enjoying their after-dinner seista, when they were roused by the neighing of Villa's stallion.

"Some one's coming," cried The Tiger, leaping to

his feet and rushing to the mouth of the cave.

Quickly his men, rifles in hand, joined him. And as they peered down the trail, they cried out in amazement as they recognized the uniform of the Rurales.

"Madre di Dios! but the curs have keener noses for the scent than I thought," exclaimed Villa.

"But they should know better than to track The Tiger to his lair.

"It will prove costly to them.

"We'll give them a leaden greeting."

As he spoke, Villa threw his rifle to his shoulder and fired.

The man in the van of the pursuers pitched from his saddle.

"Quick! Scatter into the brush!" shouted Don Sebastian.

But before the Rurales and cowpunchers could obey, five more of their number were shot.

Returning the bandits' fire as best they could while seeking places of safety, the avengers, once they reached them, opened a withering fire upon the mouth of the cave.

Before the deluge of lead, Villa realized it was folly to expose his men, and he ordered them to retreat into the cave out of the angle of fire.

This, however, was no easy matter to accomplish because the cowboys and Rurales had so spread out in extended formation that they were able to send shots into the bandits' retreat from many directions.

Undaunted, however, The Tiger bade his men to save their fire and not to expose themselves.

"We'll get them after dark," he declared. "The Rurales never fight at night. They'd rather sleep."

But in this prophecy the bandit chieftain was mistaken.

Kindling huge bonfires in a semicircle between themselves and the mouth of the cave, they were able to see any one who should emerge from it, while they themselves were shielded by the screen of flame.

Quickly recognizing the cleverness of the scheme, Villa realized that unless he devised some way of outwitting his besiegers he and his men would be in desperate straits, for the cave was not stocked with provisions, and he was not supplied with more than the ordinary amount of ammunition carried by outlaws.

His men also realized the seriousness of their position.

"How would it be a risk to dash from the cave?" suggested Tomasso.

"You'd only pay for it with your life," Villa answered. "Towards morning, perhaps, the fires will die down and then we might have a chance. But not now."

The besiegers, however, took very good care not to let the bonfires get low and sunrise found the outlaws still cooped up in their cave.

Their plight, however, was more serious because their supply of water had been exhausted.

The firing into the cave was practically abandoned by the Rurales, only an ocasional shot, as a sort of reminder that they were on the job, being sent into it.

"Something's got to be done," exclaimed Dato, when afternoon found the situation unchanged. "I'm almost dead for a drink of water."

"Me, too," declared several of the others.

A long time they discussed various plans, only to give them up as unfeasible, while The Tiger sat with his head down.

For once, his usual resourcefulness seemed to have failed him.

As though sensing the fact his men grew restless and openly cursed their fate at being imprisoned without food or water.

When twilight came, and the bonfires again blazed up, the men were on the verge of revolt.

"Are you going to get us out of here or are you going to let us die of starvation and thirst?" demanded Baptista of the bandit chieftain.

"Why?" drawled Villa, looking at him.

"Because if you're not going to do anything, I am."

"What?"

"I'm going to surrender to the Rurales."

The audacity of the fellow amazed the others and they looked at their leader to see how he would take the open defiance.

But he only smiled.

"Do you want to surrender?"

"Well, I don't want to starve to death."

"Have you forgotten your oath?"

"But you can't do anything for us. What is the use of dooming eight men to death? You can starve if you want to. The Rurales won't do anything much to us because it's you they are after."

"So it's hunger that is making you willing to violate your oath of allegiance to me and surrender to the Rurales?"

"Yes, that is, hunger and thirst together."

In open-eyed amazement the other outlaws had listened to the dialogue between their master and his minion and they wondered if The Tiger had lost his courage to brook such defiance.

But their wonder was quickly satisfied.

Sneeringly Villa stared at Baptista, then at last he spoke:

"Well, if it's hunger and thirst that are causing you to turn traitor to me, they won't trouble you long."

And whipping out his six-shooter with a lightning move, The Tiger dropped the man who had dared defy him in his tracks.

CHAPTER XIII.

A Desperate Ruse.

The drastic punishment meted out to the bandit who was willing to surrender rather than suffer privation served as an object lesson to the other outlaws, and they ceased their grumbling.

"Throw the traitor out," commanded the bandit-chieftain.

Instantly Dato and Bepo went to the body, picked it up, carried it to the mouth of the cave and threw it out.

And as it sailed through the air a volley of shots from the besiegers greeted it.

"Any more of you want to surrender?" The Tiger demanded, as Dato and Pepo rejoined him, looking from one to another of his seven remaining men.

But no one spoke.

"Good!" their master ejaculated. "I know I've been caught unprepared for once, and because of that I deem it my duty to relieve your suffering.

"If you men will remain in the cave till sunrise, I promise to get you both food and water.

"What do you say?"

Whether from fear of a fate similar to that meted out to Baptista or because they believed in their leader, the bandits all declared their readiness to remain.

"Good." Dato, I put you in command. If any man tries to desert, drop him like the cur he is.

"If I am not back by sunrise, however, you may consider yourselves released from your oaths and can do as you please."

As he finished speaking, Villa took his knife and six-shooters from their holsters and examined them carefully, then made his way to the rear of the cave and began to work at a small aperture.

"But that will take you into the bears' den," protested Bepo, as he realized his master's purpose.

For the cave in which they were entrapped derived

its name from the fact that part of it was a den of the vicious Sierra Madre bears.

"What of it?" Villa demanded.

"Why, you may stumble onto a bear," returned Bepo.

"Which is exactly what I hope to do," the bandit-chieftain replied.

Wondering if he had gone crazy, several of his men, nevertheless, helped enlarge the opening till at last Villa was able to squeeze into it.

"Bring a torch," he commanded, and when it was given him, he thrust it into the den.

"Fine. Here's a monster bear," he exclaimed. " 'Rico, hold the torch." And thrusting it into the bandit's hand, their fearless leader dropped into the den.

The sound of his striking the floor of the cave roused the bear.

Rising to his hind legs, he rushed at The Tiger.

Whipping out his shooting irons, Villa emptied their cylinders into the beast.

But the only effect they seemed to have was to make the bear roar with pain.

On the brute came and in a trice the bandit chieftain was locked in its embrace.

Furiously the bear hugged him, the while snapping at his face and tearing at his legs with its feet.

Fascinated by the terrible struggle, the bandits

peered through the opening, unable to shoot because of fear they would hit their master.

But only for a few moments were they inactive.

"Come on, we'll go down and attack the bear from behind," exclaimed Tomasso.

And quickly he and Dato were in the den.

"You go on the right side and I'll go on the left," Tomasso cried. "Put your six-shooter in the bear's ear and empty the cylinder."

Quickly they carried out the move.

For a moment he had seemed to have no effect, then the bear staggered and fell to the floor, bringing Villa down with him.

It was but the work of a few minutes for the bandits to release their master, and he got to his feet uninjured, save for scratches.

"That was a close call," he exclaimed. "I'd figured on being able to use my knife if my lead failed to stop the brute.

"As long as I live, I'll remember the assistance you two men rendered me.

"Now help me skin the bear."

Setting to the task, it was not long before it was finished.

"I'm going to put the hide on," The Tiger declared, "and you two must lace me up."

This task was also duly accomplished, the hide being

held on by a rope wound 'round and 'round the bandit chieftain's body.

As the outlaws realized their master's ruse, they gasped at his daring and watched him with admiration as he lumbered from the cave.

Scarcely had he disappeared, however, than a shot rang out.

For among the men whom Villa had refused to accept as a member of his band was one who knew of the existence of the bear's den.

Accordingly he told Don Sebastian about it, and the captain of the Rurales stationed a guard near enough to watch it, and it was this guard who had shot at what he supposed to be a bear as The Tiger emerged from the cave.

But the fellow's aim was poor, thanks to the fright the sudden appearance of the monster gave him, and Villa was not injured.

Dropping to all fours, the bandit chieftain lumbered off among the rocks, while the guard fled in the opposite direction.

The shot had been heard by the other guards, and they ran to learn the cause, fearing a sortie by the outlaws.

When the frightened guard told them he had only shot at a bear, however, they cursed him and returned to their posts at the mouth of the cave.

Making his way with the utmost caution and, perforce, slowly, Villa skirted the flank of the Rurales and got behind them.

Working in carefully, he finally succeeded in locating the grub chest.

Opening it, he gathered all he could carry and returned to the den, making his entrance at a time when the guard was at the end of his beat farthest from the den.

Hurriedly depositing the food, the daring bandit leader again went forth and returned with two pails of water, likewise filched from the commissary of the besiegers.

When he was safely inside the den for the second time, Villa clambered to the opening into the cave above and called his men.

As they reached the hole, he dropped back and handed up first the water and then the food, finally going up himself, carrying the skin that his ruse might not be discovered if any of the Rurales entered the cave.

CHAPTER XIII.

The Escape.

The food and the water so daringly obtained restored the spirits of the besieged outlaws and they laughed heartily over the exploit of their master.

Suddenly Tomasso exclaimed: "Why can't we escape through the bears' den to-night, Pancho?"

"When the cook goes to his grub chest in the morning he will know it has been raided. Then the incident of the bear coming from the cave will be remembered, and I am sure Don Sebastian is clever enough to realize that what his guard shot at was not a real bear.

"Consequently there will be a heavy guard maintained over the den from that time on."

"I believe you're right," returned the bandit chieftain.

"How about the women? Won't they raise the alarm?" asked Bepo.

"Not if we gag them," Villa replied. "As soon as we finish eating, we'll go."

Quickly their preparations were made. Betty and Miss Wales were gagged, and the bandits descended into the bears' den.

"I'll get into the hide again and take care of the guard," exclaimed The Tiger.

Quickly the skin was adjusted for the second time, and Villa lumbered forth.

Like all Mexicans, the guard hated night duty because it meant he must keep awake. Consequently as his post was out of sight of the other guards he deemed it his privilege to sleep if he could, and he was leaning against a tree, snoring, when The Tiger left the cave.

Making his way carefully, Villa reached him.

Quickly he thrust a gag in his mouth.

With all his strength the guard sought to throw off his strange captor, but he was no match for the bandit chieftain, and in due course was securely bound, hand and foot, and lashed to the tree.

That the besiegers might have a key to the method of his escape, The Tiger doffed the bear skin and left it beside the helpless guard and then returned to the den.

Passing the word for his men to come out, he led the way around the Rurales to the gulch in which their horses were hobbled.

As the besiegers had gathered up the bandits' ponies, they had no difficulty in picking out their own mounts, which they quickly did, for, thinking it impossible for Villa and his band to escape from the cave, Don Sebastian had not deemed it necessary to place a guard over the horses.

Mounting quickly, the bandits rode off down the trail.

"I wish we could give them a shot just to let them know we're out of the cave," exclaimed Felix.

But though to do so would also have delighted The Tiger, he realized the folly of such an act.

"If we do, we'll have them on our heels," he declared. "If we don't, it will be daylight or later before the curs discover we've gone and we can put miles between ourselves and them by that time."

And accordingly they rode away in silence.

Striking off on a cross trail, Villa avoided appearing on the prairie and sunrise found them in a fertile valley.

"I'm going to get rid of those women," announced Villa as they ate a breakfast from the remains of the stolen food. "Just at present they are in the way."

"Oh, what's the use of killing them," protested Bepo.

"Who said anything about killing them?" The Tiger demanded.

"Then what are you going to do with them?" asked 'Rico.

"Take them back to Los Rodas."

In amazed silence, the others heard this announcement.

"You'll be going to Los Rodas once too often," declared Tomasso. "Better turn them loose and let them go by themselves."

This, however, Villa refused to do and when evening came, selecting Dato and Tomasso as his companions, he set forth with Betty and Miss Wales.

"Where are you taking us now?" demanded the former.

"You'll know when you get there," the bandit chieftain snarled. "If you ask any more questions, I'll gag you."

This threat silenced the girls and they spoke no more.

As they reached the plains, Villa ordered Tomasso to blindfold them, for it suited his fancy to make them think that he was removing them to another retreat.

Arrived in sight of the temporary buildings that had been erected on the ruins of those he had burned, The Tiger drew rein.

"Set the girls on the ground," he commanded. And when this had been done, he continued: "I'm sorry, my dears, but the time has come for us to part. I'll just take a good-bye kiss and then leave you. You'll be able to make your way somewhere." And though Betty and Miss Wales struggled desperately, he kissed each full on the mouth, and then removed the handkerchiefs from their eyes.

For a moment the girls stared about them in bewilderment.

"Why it's Los Rodas!" suddenly cried Miss Wales.

"Exactly," chuckled the bandit chieftain. "Give my love to all the folks and tell them we're liable to call again any time.

"And now good-bye. We've enjoyed your company immensely."

And sweeping off his sombrero he bowed in mock deference, laughed sneeringly and galloped away, while the girls ran to the temporary ranch house.

CHAPTER XIV.

VILLA LEVIES TRIBUTE.

When day broke after the escape of the bandits from the bear cave, the cook started to prepare breakfast.

Lifting the lid of the grub chest, he stared at its almost emptiness, then gave a yell that brought the Rurales hurrying to him.

Quickly he explained to the captain the loss of the food.

"Yes, and two of my water pails are gone," he cried.

Just then the guard who had gone to relieve the one on duty at the bear's den shouted an alarm as he came upon the bound and gagged body of his fellow.

When Don Sebastian reached there and heard the guard's report of being attacked, the bear skin explained the situation to him.

"Pancho is sure some clever devil," he exclaimed, compelled to admiration of the manner in which the bandit chieftain had escaped from what seemed certain capture.

"But perhaps they haven't all gone," suggested one of his men.

Shots fired into the cave without being answered seemed to prove the contrary, however, though the Rurales were not positive until the loss of the horses was reported.

"It will be a long time before we have The Tiger in so tight a place again," lamented Don Sebastian. Then he gave the order to break camp, and once again the Rurales took up the search for the bandit chieftain.

For several days Villa and his men rested in the ravine to which they had come from the bear's cave.

"What we need is money," he announced one morning. "I want to go to Pampas and try my luck with the cards and it takes money to gamble."

"What's it going to be, bank, train or ranch robbery?" asked Rambo. "I know a rancher who always keeps three or four thousand dollars in gold in his safe."

"Not enough," returned The Tiger.

"How about Senor Gonzales' bank, in Casas Grandes?" asked 'Rico. "It is very rich and, I could also, perhaps, bring away the Senorita Dolores."

"We're going to cut out the women for a while," his master returned. "Gonzales' bank may be rich, but it is also in a town, and just at present I don't think towns are particularly safe places for Francisco Villa."

"Then what is it?" inquired Tomasso, never seeming to fear the wrath of his master for asking leading questions. "How much do you want, anyway?"

"Oh, about fifty thousand dollars."

"Say, you're no piker, at all events," Tomasso replied in admiration of the man who would not be satisfied with a raid which netted him less than such a sum. "Where on earth do you expect to pick up such a bundle at one time?"

The evident flattery in his minion's words and tone gratified The Tiger's vanity, and he grinned and chuckled in delight.

"There are rich mines in Honoros," he said, "and

once a week they send the ore wagons from the mines
to the railroad at Las Palmos."

"But they are always sent under a heavy escort,"
declared Felix, while the others stared at the man
who was daring enough even to think of attacking
one of the rich prizes.

"Eight men who are not afraid are more than a
match for fifty with faint hearts," exclaimed the
bandit chieftain. "There are eight of us but there are
not fifty guards sent with the ore wagons.

"Usually only three wagons are sent out and there
are four guards to each wagon, which with the
drivers, makes fifteen men all told."

"But the guards are Gringos, not Mexicans," declared Rambo.

"Is a Gringo's heart any stouter than a Mexican's?"
snapped The Tiger.

"No, of course not."

"Then what difference does it make whether the
guards are Mexicans or Gringos?"

"None at all," returned the outlaw, realizing that
he had made a mistake in disparaging the courage of
the peons.

"I'm glad you realize it," Villa retorted and lapsed
into a sullen silence.

"Do any of you happen to know the days on which

the ore wagons leave the mines?" he finally asked.

None of his band did, however.

"Then we must go and camp on the trail till we learn the lay of the land," he announced. "Therefore, the sooner we start, the better.

"We'll set out tonight."

The contemplated raid upon the wagons, rich with gold and silver bullion, furnished the outlaws with a topic of conversation throughout the day, and it was with impatience that they awaited the coming of darkness.

Riding close to the mountains, the bandits travelled for the most part by night, and rested under the cover of the woods by day.

As their supply of food was running low, it became necessary to replenish it.

So Villa headed for Los Remedios ranch.

It was mid-day when the eight bandits reached it.

Riding up to the door of the house, The Tiger beat upon it with the butt of his six-shooter.

"Is Senor Benton at home?" he asked of the servant who came to the door.

"No."

"Expect him soon?"

"Not till night."

"Where are the punchers?"

"Riding the range."

Made easy by this information, the wily bandit realized that he must not show his gratification.

"Well, is anybody home but you?" he inquired, petulantly.

"Yes, Mrs. Benton is."

"Then, may I see her?"

"Who shall I say?"

"A gentleman."

Closing the door, for the appearance of the bandit chieftain and his companions was anything but prepossessing, the servant went to her mistress and reported the interview.

Mindful of the raids upon neighboring ranches, Mrs. Benton went to a window in the front room and raised it.

"What do you wish?" she asked of The Tiger.

"Dinner for myself and men."

"But the cook is on the range. I cannot give it to you."

For several moments Villa stared at the woman, then exclaimed:

"Madam, you *must* give us dinner."

The owner of Los Remedios was one of the wealthiest men in Mexico, and such language to his wife was an insult which she hotly resented.

"Who are you to tell me I *must* do anything?" she demanded angrily.

In mock deference, The Tiger swept off his sombrero and bowed low in his saddle, exclaiming:

"I am Francisco Villa—at your service, madam."

The name of the terrible bandit caused Mrs. Benton to blanch, and she clutched the window sash.

"I see you have heard of me," The Tiger continued. "Will you give us dinner?"

"Er—yes, that is, if you will eat it in the shack."

"Impossible, madam. We will either eat at your table or——" and he paused significantly.

"Or what?" asked Mrs. Benton faintly.

"Or I am afraid you will have neither table nor house to put it in for supper."

"You mean you will burn our home?"

"Madam's grasp of the situation is perfect."

A moment the wife of the owner of Los Remedios hesitated, then said:

"Very well, I will call you when it is ready."

And as she turned away, Villa laughed jeeringly.

With his dinner, the bandit chieftain demanded wine, and the amount he and his men consumed before he left the ranch made a big hole in Benton's cellar.

When at last The Tiger thought it time to be moving, he said:

"Now, if you will bring your jewels, Mrs. Benton, we will leave."

Her fear of her unwelcome guests rising, as they consumed more and more wine, she lost no time in going to her room and returning with a small jewel box.

"These are all I have," she said, handing the case to Villa. Then, as he frowned upon seeing only a few pieces, she added, hastily

"You see, I keep most of my jewels in the city. It is safer."

"That is not what I have heard," The Tiger replied. "I fear I must look for myself."

Heedless of Mrs. Benton's protests, Villa made his way to her room and soon returned with a diamond necklace about his throat and a sunburst on his bosom.

"I will take these to remember the delightful day we have had," he sneered, and to the great relief of Mrs. Benton, took his departure, carrying with him a small fortune in gems.

CHAPTER XV.

A $50,000 Haul.

"'Won't old Benton be wild when he returns and learns I've levied tribute on Los Remedios?" chuckled the bandit chieftain as he and his men galloped on their way.

"I'd surely like to see the old aristocrat's face when his wife tells him.

"I've a good mind to go back and wait for him."

As the outlaws heard these words, they were dismayed. The number of punchers employed by Benton was very large, and a score or more of them might ride up at any moment, and they were of different calibre from the cowboys of Los Rodas. Therefore a return to the ranch might spell direst disaster to them.

But they all were aware of their master's disposition when he had been drinking and deemed it best not to attempt to dissuade him.

"Yes," announced Villa, drawing rein," I think we will go back."

"I thought you wanted money and lots of it," exclaimed Tomasso, in a desperate attempt to turn the determination, by appealing to his chief's covetousness.

"So I do."

"Well, there are only a few dollars at Los Remedios, compared to what you'll get from the ore wagons."

As the bandit played this trump card his companions watched anxiously the effect it would have upon The Tiger.

For several moments that seemed ages to them, Villa considered. But at last he spoke.

"I believe you are right, Tomasso," he said.

"There's no believe about it. I know I am," the outlaw replied.

"All right, we'll keep going then," exclaimed Villa.

And many were the sighs of relief the bandits gave as they resumed their forward way.

When dawn came they again took to the woods, and Villa removed the diamonds, putting them in his pocket, but each night as they set forth on their ride, he put the necklace about his throat and pinned the sunburst to the bosom of his shirt.

Arrived at last on the outskirts of Los Palmos, Villa ordered his men to separate and ride into the town in pairs at intervals of an hour and further instructed them not to know one another.

"They may be suspicious of so many strangers," he said, "and it won't do to arouse any suspicion."

"I'll take Tomasso with me. We'll look over the route to the mines, find the best place to attack the wagons, and what day they leave the mines.

"When I'm ready, you'll see me ride through the main street at noon with a red bandanna about my neck.

"Everybody understand?"

"What shall we say we are, if anybody asks?" inquired Felix.

"Cow punchers. But don't let anybody ask you if you can help it.

"Anything else?"

None of them had any more questions to ask and, nodding to Tomasso, the bandit chieftain rode into Los Palmos.

The next morning bright and early Villa and his companion set out for the mines in Honoras.

Had any one else been travelling the road, they would have been surprised by the sight of two men every now and then jumping their horses into the brush beside the trail, and at other times mounting rocks and looking up and down the road.

Arrived at the mines, The Tiger announced themselves as cowboys with a desire to see what mines looked like, and their every wish in that respect was granted, their guide even going so far as to give them the much desired information that the ore wagons left the mines at four o'clock on Monday morning in time to load the ore onto cars which were hauled from Los Palmos at five in the afternoon.

"I suppose they are heavily guarded," commented the bandit chieftain.

"You just bet they are," assented the miner who was showing them about," fifteen men all told, including the three drivers, and each guard has three rifles besides two six-shooters.

"And those fellows are some shots, too, and don't you forget it. There isn't one of them who can't put a bullet through an ace of diamonds at a hundred feet."

"Which is sure some shooting," The Tiger acquiesced.

Having completed the rounds, the two bandits rode away.

"I'm not so certain of our eight men being a match

for those twelve guards if they are such expert shots and have three rifles apiece."

"It's a cinch, man dear."

"How do you figure that?"

"Why, shoot them each in the right arm. It'll take quick work, but we'll have the jump on them."

As they returned to the railroad town, the two outlaws decided that a turn in the road, protected by bushes on the inside would be the place to commit the hold-up.

"It will be daylight when they get to it," announced Villa, "and we shall be able to shoot the guards from the bushes without their seeing us or knowing how many of us there are."

"It'll be some stunt," Tomasso declared. "But how are we going to carry the stuff away? Bullion is heavy stuff."

"We'll just take what we can carry and leave the rest. It's a shame but we'll have to."

Having thus worked out the details of the hold-up, Villa and Tomasso rode into Los Palmos.

As it was then a Friday, they were only obliged to idle away two days.

In the most casual way Villa managed to chat with his other men and tell them to meet him at the curve in the road by nine o'clock on Monday morning, thus obviating the necessity of his riding through the town with the red bandanna about his neck.

At the appointed hour, the eight bandits met at the turn in the road.

Calculating that the wagons would be along about ten, The Tiger took his men into the brush and stationed them at intervals of twenty feet.

"We'll have to kill some of them, of course," he exclaimed, "but try for their right arms first.

"If you can put a bullet into them, the Gringos won't be able to use their rifles.

"Remember not to show yourselves till I give the word."

Having received their instructions the bandits awaited with what patience they could the coming of the ore wagons.

At last the creaking of the bodies under the heavy ore reached their ears.

Intently each outlaw peered through the leaves, a six-shooter in each hand. For it had been one of Villa's requirements of the men he recruited that they could shoot equally well with either hand.

Nearer and nearer came the sound of the wagons.

At last the horses of the first wagon rounded the turn.

But there was no one on it save the driver.

The second wagon also appeared without any guard, but when the third one hove in sight some of the twelve men were stretched out on it, chatting and laughing, while others were playing guards.

Such a breach of their instructions would have brought a severe reprimand from any of the officers of the mine had they seen it, but the guards, having traversed the route so many times without any misadventure, had become careless.

When the last wagon had reached a spot opposite to where he and Tomasso were stationed, Villa opened fire.

Instantly the other bandits followed suit.

Dumfounded at the suddenness of the attack, for an instant the guards were motionless, then such of them as could slid over the farther side of the wagon and made for their proper stations, for they had left their rifles on their wagons.

Therefore there were only three guns to be turned against the bandits.

The firing by the outlaws was incessant.

Two of the guards on the third wagon dropped, shot to death, while the shooting arm of the third member was put out of commission.

As the other guards, protected for the moment by the sides of the wagons, put up their hands to get their rifles, the bandits sent shots into the arms of all but two.

These men were clever enough to call to the drivers

to throw out their rifles, and then to run their horses for all they were worth to the railroad station.

Catching the guns as they were tossed to them the two guards dashed back to the third wagon and, hiding as much of their bodies behind it as they could, opened fire into the bushes.

The first shot, fired at random as it was, found Felix, and he tumbled from his horse.

Next Bepo's mount was shot.

Then Rambo fell.

At last, however, the magazines of the rifles they carried were empty and they were obliged to stop firing.

"Give us your extra guns," called one of the men in the cart.

Powerless to use their right hands, they were able to hand them out with their left, and again a rain of lead was poured into the bushes.

Two bullets found Villa, and Pulque's horse was shot from under him.

Realizing that the toll they were paying was heavy, The Tiger leaned toward Tomasso.

"When their magazines are empty again, we'll jump into the road and drill them full of lead.

"If we're quick we can do it before they get fresh rifles."

With the cessation of bullets, Villa and his companion leaped their horses from the brush and emptied the cylinders of their six-shooters into the guards, dropping both of them.

"Come out, you men!" yelled the bandit chieftain to those of his fellows still in the bushes.

Quickly they obeyed but before they gained the road, Tomasso had bound the drivers at his master's command.

"Now the sacks," The Tiger exclaimed as he drew his own from the bosom of his shirt.

"Everybody, up onto the wagon, and help yourselves! Don't bother with the silver. Just take all the gold you can carry."

Hastily the outlaws put the blocks of gold into their bags.

"I hate to leave so much," lamented Bepo.

"Never mind, if it takes a wagon to carry it all, we can't take but a little," returned Villa.

At last every bandit was loaded to his capacity.

"Get your horses and ride for it," commanded The Tiger. "It's every man for himself now.

"I'll manage to meet you if possible at the ravine in about six months."

And clapping spurs to his stallion, Villa raced through the woods, Dato and Tomasso by his side.

As he rode away, The Tiger rose in his saddle.

"If any one asks you who did this," he shouted, "tell them it was Francisco Villa!"

CHAPTER XVI.

VILLA PAYS AN EVENING CALL.

Pulque and Bepo, having lost their mounts, took the horses of Felix and Rambo, who had been killed, and made their getaway riding together, while 'Rico went off by himself.

The toll of the fight had been heavy, two out of eight of the bandits killed, the other six all wounded; of the fifteen ore guards, five were killed and all the others shot in the right arm.

Only the driver was uninjured and he was bound and helpless.

Having hauled the first two ore wagons out of range of the guns, the drivers halted.

Unharnessing one of his horses, the man on the first wagon leaped onto its back and dashed for Los Palmos to summon aid.

Ere he returned, however, the bandits had put miles between themselves and the scene of this fifty-thousand-dollar haul, as it was a good twelve miles from the town to the stalled wagons, and the horse was a heavy Percheron.

While they waited the coming of assistance, the guards on the third wagon managed with their left hands to loosen the driver's bonds and he in turn helped them bind up their wounds.

In due course the Rurales and many townsfolk arrived, but though they took up the trails they never saw the bandits.

This hold-up added the finishing touch to the terror that the name of the bandit chieftain inspired.

Men and women asked each other what he would do next and bankers and train officials increased the guards over their money and money shipments, while ranch owners laid in fresh supplies of firearms and ammunition.

When the news of this latest outrage perpetrated

by The Tiger reached President Diaz, in Mexico
City, he immediately offered an additional prize of
ten thousand dollars for the bandit's capture, and sent
instructions that the force of Rurales on his trail be
doubled.

But neither the head money nor the Rurales
bothered Villa. In fact, they bore testimony to the
fear in which he was held and thus gratified his
vanity.

But despite the success of the hold-up, the bandit
chieftain really had a white elephant on his hands.

The gold he had stolen was bullion.

If he took it anywhere to be exchanged for coin,
he would be recognized and possibly shot. Nor could
he delegate the task of exchanging the bullion for
coin to his men, and this because anyone presenting
any bullion with such a request would be certain to
be arrested and the gold would be confiscated.

When the three bandits realized this, they were
puzzled as to what to do.

"Why not go to the States?" suggested Dato.

"The risk there would be the same as here. We'd
be arrested."

"South America?" Tomasso proposed.

"Too far. Besides," returned his master, "I don't
see why I should be obliged to leave Mexico to change
this gold.

"And what's more, I won't!" And he brought his fist down against the palm of his left hand with a resounding whack.

"What will you do, then?" inquired Tomasso.

"I'll show you tonight."

When darkness fell, the three bandits were on the outskirts of Casas Grandes.

Hobbling their horses in the woods, they made their way on foot into the town.

"Where does Senor Gonzales, the banker live?" he asked of the first peon he met, and having received the information, went to the banker's house.

"I wish to see the Senor," he told the servant who answered his summons.

"Say it is about a large loan."

Fortunately for the success of his request, Villa stood in the shadow and the servant could not see how shabbily he was dressed for a man desiring a large loan.

In quick order the banker appeared.

"What can I do for you?" he asked, looking from one to the other of the trio.

Like a flash, The Tiger whipped out his six-shooter, and covered the banker.

"You can do this—come to your bank with us now," he snapped.

"This is monstrous!" Gonzales protested.

"Either come or go to your death," growled Villa, "but be quick about your decision, we haven't any time to waste."

"I-I will go," assented the banker.

"Good. Now, don't make any outcry on the street. If you do, I'll shoot you, for I shall have my gun on you as we walk along. Come on."

And pressing the muzzle of his revolver against Gonzales' side he kept step with the thoroughly terrified banker.

Arrived at the bank, Gonzales was so frightened he could scarcely unlock the door. Bnt at last he succeeded, and they entered.

"What now?" he asked, his teeth chattering.

"Here's a candle," and The Tiger drew one from his pocket. "Light it. Then open your safe. I want to exchange some bullion for gold coin."

At the request, the banker almost dropped the candle, so terrified was he, for he knew he was in the power of the terrible bandit chieftain.

"You are Francisco Villa?" he stammered.

"I'm not saying who I am," the outlaw returned. "Just get busy. My time is valuable."

After much fumbling, due to his nervousness, the banker opened the safe, and as Villa saw the money in the vault, his eyes danced.

Producing five bars of gold, he handed them to Gonzales.

"Coin for that," he snapped," and mind you, don't cheat on the weight."

The words put an idea in the banker's head, and he short-weighted The Tiger and his two companions, who also produced five bars of gold each.

When they had received the coin in exchange, Villa turned on Gonzales.

"I think from your face that you have cheated us. No aristocrat can cheat Francisco Villa.

"To be on the safe side, we'll just take some of this money in the vault.

"Help yourself, Dato, and you, Tomasso."

Quickly, the three bandits took all the gold they could, while the banker wrung his hands and wailed that he was ruined.

Unable to carry more of the precious metal, The Tiger turned on Gonzales.

"Let this be a lesson to you not to cheat people you deal with," he snapped. "Thank you for your service to us—you aristocrat."

And as he passed the banker, Villa spat in his face.

CHAPTER XVII.

The Tiger Lifts the Lid.

"I'll bet old Gonzales never will get over this," The Tiger chuckled, as he and his companions reached the street. "Also, I don't believe he'll cheat any more customers for a long time."

"Where to now?" asked Tomasso, as they swung into their saddles.

"To Pampas and the cards. We've got the money now and I'm going to lift the lid off that town."

The idea appealed to Villa's companions, and in high spirits they arrived at Pampas in due time.

The one street of the town was lined with dance halls, saloons and gambling dens.

Going up to a man standing in front of one of the drinking places the bandit chieftain asked:

"Where do they play the highest stakes?"

"At the 'Yellow Dog.'"

And thither the trio went.

Entering the den, in which men and women were dancing, drinking and gambling, Villa went from one game to another, finally stopping at the roulette wheel.

Ignorant of the manner in which the game was played, he watched for a while.

Suddenly he put his hand in his pocket, drew it out full of double eagles and slapped them down on the double O.

"Are you playing that?" asked the man at the wheel.

"How much do I get?"

"Thirty-four to one."

"Sounds good. Yes, I'm playing it returned The Tiger.

Grinning broadly, the man at the wheel spun the marble, while the other players stopped for the moment to watch the stranger.

Round and round spun the marble, then slower till it began to bump against the partitions.

Of all the onlookers, Villa was the most unconcerned.

Finally, with a "chuck," the marble rolled into the double O.

"Luck seems to be with me tonight," The Tiger laughed as the banker with great reluctance counted the amount of Villa's bet and paid him $4800.

"Instead of taking any of his winnings the bandit chieftain let them lie on the cloth.

"Playing this time?" inquired the man at the wheel.

"Spin the marble and I'll see."

"Have to place your bet before I start it."

"All right. Put it on 17."

Again the marble spun round, and again it dropped in the number Villa was playing.

Cursing to himself the banker again paid the 34 to 1 winning.

"Let's have some wine for the house," exclaimed the bandit chieftain.

While waiting for it, Villa turned his attention to the women.

An unusually pretty girl attracted his eye, and quickly he beckoned her to him.

"I'll play some of this gold for you, beauty," he said.

The arrival of the wine stopped all play for the moment while every one in the den drank the lavish stranger's health.

Word of The Tiger's winnings had spread to the other dives and men and women were flocking in to see the excitement.

Among them came the proprietor of the "Yellow Dog," who deemed it best to be present when such high play was going on.

"Any limit to this game?" the terrible outlaw asked when the wheel again started.

In answer the banker looked at the owner of the dive.

"Nothing but the sky," that worthy returned.

"Suits me to a 'T,' " The Tiger grinned. "I came to Pampas to lift the lid and I don't think I can lift it any higher than the sky.

"Here, beauty, I'll play half of this for you, if you want."

Eagerly the girl accepted.

Again Villa put all his previous winnings on one number, this time returning to the double O.

"I'd rather have my half now," exclaimed the girl, in disgust as she saw the bandit's play.

"You shall have it, win or lose," he answered.

Round the roulette table men and women were jammed till they could hardly move, each and every one watching the lucky stranger.

"Any one else going to play?" asked the man at the wheel, but no one cared to back his choice against Villa's.

When the marble rolled into double O, the beauty threw her arms round The Tiger's neck.

"Can I really have half?" she asked.

"Sure thing. Didn't I say so?" Then turning to the banker, he said, "Come, hurry up. I want to dance a while."

But the banker only looked at the owner of the "Yellow Dog," and shook his head.

"Come on, hurry up. Have you grown deaf?" The Tiger demanded. "I want my money."

Of all those in the den, Villa and his companions were the only ones who did not understand the situation.

"Don't you get it?" asked the beauty. "They *can't* pay you—you've broken the bank."

For several moments Villa stared dumbly at the girl, then at last the truth dawned on him.

Whirling, he seized the owner of the "Yellow Dog" by the coat lapel and jerked him from the crowd.

"Is that true—you can't pay me my winnings?" hissed The Tiger, his face distraught with fury.

"Jake says it is," returned the gambler, putting the onus on his banker.

"But you told me the sky was the limit. Yet that pile of gold isn't four inches high and you can't pay it."

"I can if you'll give me time."

"Sure I'll give you time—just five minutes."

As he uttered the words, which meant ruin to the "Yellow Dog," the lights went out.

Instantly there was a wild scramble for Villa's gold, which still lay on the table, by the human dregs who had flocked into the dive.

"Light those lamps again," thundered Villa. "If anybody touches my gold, I'll search every mother's whelp of you."

And to emphasize his words, The Tiger pulled his six-shooters and sent a couple of shots into the ceiling.

At the bark of the guns, the lights flashed up again. On the roulette table lay pieces of gold where the thieves had dropped them.

"I've got the jump on you now," yelled the bandit chieftain. Then turning, he placed one of his shooters against the owner of the "Yellow Dog's" heart.

"If you douse those glims again or try any more funny tricks, "The Tiger shouted, "I'll send a dose of lead into this man.

"Get me? Good. And now I want my winnings. "Shell out."

"But we can't pay you," protested the banker.

"Then give me what you've got.

"Tomasso, go round behind the table and see he doesn't fool me."

"He can't do that," protested the "Yellow Dog" owner.

"Don't tell me what he can do and what he can't," snarled Villa, jabbing with his gun barrel.

The hint was sufficient, and in silence they all watched while Tomasso joined the banker.

"We're ten thousand short," the banker announced.

"Get it," demanded Villa, whirling on his captive.

"I can give you, five of it."

"I believe your lying. Dato, come here and search this Gringo."

Obeying, it did not take long for the bandit to produce a roll of money which counted up to twelve thousand dollars.

"Trying to welch on me, weren't you?" hissed The Tiger. "Take it all, Dato.

"I'll teach the pale-faced pig to try to play tricks on Francisco Villa!"

At the name a gasp of terror ran through the den.

"Got the money, Tomasso?" The Tiger called.

"Yes."

"Then come on. And you, you piker, can consider yourself lucky to get off with your life." And he shook the "Yellow Dog" owner, then sent him spinning from him.

A couple of paces Villa took toward the door, then stopped.

"Here, girlie, where are you?" he called, and as

the beauty approached, he continued: "I'd almost forgotten you.

"Tomasso has my winnings, but I guess this will be equal to half of them." And putting his hand in his pouch, the bandit chieftain drew it out full twice and gave it to the astonished girl. Then he kissed and made for the door.

As he reached it, some one shouted: "There's 30,000 dollars prize money on his head. Let's get it."

Instantly, Villa whirled, then dropped to the floor.

"He's been knifed!" shrieked the beauty.

CHAPTER XVIII.

BETRAYED.

Instantly Tomasso and Dato rushed to their chief and picked him up.

"Where can we take him?" exclaimed Dato.

"To my home, if you want to," declared the girl to whom he had been so generous.

"Where is it?"

"What makes you ask?"

"Because since these people know The Tiger we can't stay in Pampas."

"It isn't in Pampas."

"Is it far?"

"Forty miles. I board in town, you know."

"Good. We'll go there. Tomasso, put the girl on

your horse, I'll take Rancho on the stallion and you take mine.

"Lively now."

Quickly they moved away, and none too soon, for a score or more guns barked.

"Nice, friendly people in this town of Pampas," exclaimed Tomasso as he swung the beauty up onto his horse.

"They'd murder their mothers for a pèso," she replied.

Fortunately for the bandits, there were no other horses in front of the "Yellow Dog," or their getaway would have been more difficult.

As it was the denizens of Pampas sent bullet after bullet at them, though none took effect.

Forced to ride slowly, once they had gained the open on account of the pain The Tiger was suffering, it was after sunrise when they reached the girl's home, which proved to be only an abandoned hovel.

"My family are dead," she explained, "so I took everything and went to Pampas. My name is Mercedes Horta.

"But Pancho will be safe here. No one knows about it in Pampas."

Making their chief as comfortable as they could, Tomasso and Dato decided that the former should ride to the nearest ranch and buy provisions and medicine.

"If you don't want to get a doctor, there's an old Indian woman near here who is great on salves and such things," said Mercedes.

"Get her," ordered Dato. And as Tomasso rode away to get food, the girl sped for the medicine woman.

The old squaw examined the wound carefully, shook her head and hurried away, returning with various herbs and lotions which she applied deftly.

For three days Villa's fever raged and his chums despaired of his life, but on the fourth there was a change for the better, and from then on his improvement was rapid.

Thinking they had nothing to fear from the squaw who was paid handsomely, the others made no effort to conceal The Tiger's identity.

But bitterly were they to rue this carelessness.

When the danger was over, the old Indian went home.

Enjoying the society of Mercedes, and thinking themselves safe from all pursuit, the bandits lingered long after their chief was able to ride.

Like all Indians, the squaw was covetous. She knew there was a big reward offered for The Tiger, and she determined to get at least some of it.

So setting forth, she went to the nearest barracks of the Rurales at Esclamon and laid her information as to the whereabouts of the much-wanted bandit chieftain before the captain.

Keen was his delight as she told him, and hardly pausing to thank her, he ordered out his men.

"Hold on!" she shrieked. "How much of the reward do I get?"

"Not a peso. The money goes to those who capture Villa, not to informers," he shouted back, as he swung into his saddle.

Unbelieving, the old hag stood for a moment, then realizing that she would gain nothing from her betrayal of the man who had paid her so generously, she raised her hands above her head and shrieked:

"May the fiends of hell sit on the chest of you, your wife and your children and gnaw their hearts out! And may you die the death of the dog that you are, spurned by all your friends."

Then she staggered back to her hovel.

The bandits were lolling in the house and Mercedes was at the spring when she chanced to look up and saw a body of horsemen racing toward the hut.

"Rurales!" she gasped, and dashing for the house, she shouted: "The Rurales are coming!"

Amazed, the bandits leaped to the windows and verified the warning.

Catching Mercedes about the waist, Villa ran with her to the shack in which were their horses, followed by his chums.

No time was there to saddle, so close were the man-hunters, so the bandits merely bridled and leaped onto their mounts, The Tiger swinging the girl up in front of him.

"The only thing to do is for us each to ride in a different direction," exclaimed their leader.

"By doing that the curs won't know which of us I am.

"Meet you at the bear cave."

Quickly the outlaws raced from the shack, Villa heading north, Tomasso east, and Dato south.

As he saw them escaping, the captain of the Rurales shouted a command which divided his troop into three sections, and each one gave chase to the lone horseman ahead of it.

CHAPTER XIX.

THE REUNION.

Needless to say, the Rurales did not capture The Tiger, or Dato or Tomasso.

But from the time when the bandit chieftain dashed over the prairie, carrying Mercedes before him, the two of them dropped out of sight as completely as though the earth had swallowed them.

When a month passed and their chief did not appear at the rendezvous he had made at the bear cave, Tomasso and Dato grew anxious.

"Let's see if he's been to cache to get any more of the gold bullion," suggested Dato.

Accordingly they went to the spot where they had buried the loot obtained by robbing the ore wagons.

Villa's share of the plunder was gone, but their's was intact.

"Would he shake old chums like us for that pretty girl?" demanded Tomasso, as they sat down to discuss the discovery that The Tiger's bullion had been removed from the cache.

"You never can tell what a man will do when there's a woman in the case," said Dato, wisely, "but it doesn't seem possible."

It was not for some few years that the three bandits met again.

Where Villa passed those years is as much of a mystery as why he changed his name from Doroteo Arranzo to Francisco Villa, and like that, is probably known only to himself.

It may have been during this period that The Tiger served an enlistment. Also, he may have visited during it the old South American countries, where rumor has it, he led several revolutions.

But wherever he was, he returned sound in limb and body, and he today swears that save on the two occasions when Huerta put him there he has never been in jail.

It was in a barroom in Juarez that the three men met after the long years of separation.

Tomasso and Dato had stuck together, barely managing to keep out of the hands of the Rurales while indulging in raids that were tame compared to those led by The Tiger.

A lucky hold-up supplied the pair with funds, and they decided the States would be much safer for them for a while than Mexico.

Accordingly they went to El Paso but, as the racing season was on, they frequently crossed to Juarez.

Having passed an afternoon at the track, they dropped into the Grinning Bear saloon.

As they did so, a man who had been drinking turned about.

It was Francisco Villa.

The recognition was mutual.

"Madre di Dios, Panch——" began Dato, rushing to him with outstretched hands.

But The Tiger put his finger to his lips to enjoin silence as to his identity.

As of old, the others obeyed him and, turning on their heels, the three left the Grinning Bear and entered another barroom.

Villa, however, evaded questions as to Mercedes and what he had been doing, merely declaring that he had been able to turn a few tricks.

"But I've got something on now, old pals, in which you can help me. How about it?"

CHAPTER XX.

Villa Wreaks His Vengeance.

Only too glad to have been reunited with their old-time leader, the others eagerly declared their willingness to share any danger or pleasure with The Tiger.

"It's this way," declared the bandit chieftain: "I have a little ranch near Sonora. And I had a daughter there.

"I was not known as Francisco Villa—what the name was is of no consequence.

"I went away on a business trip.

"When I returned, I found the house but smouldering embers.

"Crazed with anxiety I started to find my little Dolores. She was six years old.

"I did not have far to search.

"In an orchard some hundred yards from where the house had been I came upon her little body hanging from a limb.

"To her dress was pinned a note. Here it is."

And from his money pouch Villa took a soiled piece of paper and read:

"'We do not want any Villas or brats of Villa's in Sonora.

"We came to get you. The girl would not tell us where you were.

"Let this be a warning to you as to what we shall do to you when we get you—and get you we will if you remain in Sonora.

'CARLOS,
'Prince of the Black Riders.'"

There were tears in the eyes of The Tiger as he finished reading the warning, and though he essayed to speak, his voice was too broken.

"So you want us to help you hunt this Carlos, Prince of Black Riders down?" said Tomasso.

"Yes," said their chief, recovering his composure. "That is, I'd be glad to have your company tonight.

"This all happened six weeks ago, but it was only

this morning I learned who Carlos was.

"He and his band of cutthroats have been away on one of what they call their vigilante trips.

"They return tonight.

"Their meeting place is in a hut in the woods five miles to the south of here.

"Carlos always comes to his home after a trip before going to the headquarters.

"I shall meet him between his home and the rendezvous."

"We're with you," chorused Tomasso and Dato.

"Good! Let's go out, I have some purchases to make."

Going to the hardware shop, The Tiger purchased a meat cleaver, two quarts of black paint and a paint brush.

"Why the——?"

"Don't ask questions," Villa interrupted. "You'll understand tonight."

In various saloons the bandits passed the time till The Tiger deemed it necessary for them to go on their mission.

Riding till they came to a group of trees, they halted and Villa uncoiled his lariat.

Hidden by the shadows they could see up and down the road without themselves being visible.

At the end of half an hour their vigil was rewarded by the appearance of a horseman garbed all in black.

Waiting till the rider was opposite The Tiger threw his lariat and jerked the horseman from the saddle.

With the assistance of his chums the bandit dragged him to the trees.

"I am Francisco Villa," he announced. "I have come to avenge my Dolores.

"And for one pain you caused her I will make you suffer a hundred.

"First I'll begin with your fingers. You'll get more agony."

Binding the man rigid with his lariat, The Tiger spread out his left hand and chopped off the fingers with his meat cleaver.

"Gag him, so he can't give any alarm by his cries, Dato," the terrible bandit commanded.

Then he chopped off the fingers of the right hand.

Next he cut the arms at the elbows.

The feet at the ankles were then severed.

Finally, the arms were cut off at the shoulders, and the legs at the groin.

Hurriedly opening the paint, The Tiger stripped the clothes from the parts of the body and painted the different pieces black.

This done, he placed them in a bag which he swung

at his saddle horn, then mounted and rode ahead, followed by his horrified chums.

Arrived at the shack, Villa dismounted and took the bag.

Going to the door of the shanty he opened it and hurled in the head.

As it rolled along the floor, hideous in its black paint, The Tiger yelled:

"Here is your Carlos, Prince of Black Riders, by order of Francisco Villa."

Then as fast as he could, he threw the other parts of the body into the room, laughed shrilly, and going to his horse, mounted and rode away.

CHAPTER XXI.

VILLA INCREASES HIS BAND.

Though they had seen their leader in many moods, and under many circumstances, never had they seen him so much like the devil incarnate, which his enemies call him, as when he was wreaking his vengeance upon the so-called "Prince of the Black Riders."

So terrible was he to behold, face, hands and clothes bespattered with the blood of his victim, that they dared not speak to him.

Accordingly they fell in behind him and followed him.

To their surprise, instead of heading for Juarez, The Tiger led them in the direction of their old stamping ground, the Sierra Madre Mountains.

Like wild fire, the news of the horrible fate to which the leader of the Black Riders had been subjected spread, and when they heard it had been inflicted by the terrible bandit chieftain, people again began to fear his raids.

And good reason did they have so to do.

The cruel death of his Dolores seemed to drown out any spark of human kindness that had been in him, leaving him all devil.

With the band which he quickly recruited—and among them were others of his old followers, Bepo, 'Rico and Pulque—he was short and firm. With his enemies, when he could catch them, he was merciless, and he took particular delight in torturing any of the Rurales who, while hunting him, chanced to fall into his hands.

Up and down the States of Durango and Chihuahua he rode, robbing, burning, murdering. His methods were the same as of yore. His appearance was as sudden and as unexpected, but he was evermore prone to shoot any one who crossed or thwarted him in any way.

The rule of his arch-enemy, Porifirio Diaz, was tottering.

The ignorant masses were becoming incensed at the wrongs to which they were subjected at the hands of the land owners and the aristocracy.

Through the country Francisco Madero was going, telling them that as human beings they had some rights, but that they could never hope to attain them till they revolted against the rule of Diaz and the reactionary forces for which he stood.

As a result of this revolutionary propaganda, the men of the masses were growing restless.

They formed into bands and began to pillage and burn, taking by force the things they could not have otherwise.

It was natural, therefore, that in this spirit of brigandage they should look to the most desperate brigand Mexico had ever known, Francisco Villa, as their leader—and they did.

Men from all sections of the country sought him out and begged him to let them ride with him. But he was ever a believer in small forces which could strike quickly and get away even more quickly.

Nevertheless, he added many of the applicants to his band, administering the old oath of allegiance to them, until it numbered about thirty.

In all truth he had made himself the people's idol and terror.

CHAPTER XXII.

The Raid on the Sonoma Colony.

Ever since the death of his daughter, The Tiger had sought to learn who it was that had disclosed his real identity to the Black Riders.

His efforts, however, had been in vain.

And in his fury, he turned from the individual to the group and began to harass the colonists at Sonoma.

At first he confined himself to running off their horses and cattle, and to burning their ranch houses.

But as they either bought more or built new ones, he conceived the idea of rendering them powerless so to do by depriving them of their money.

In the fertile Sonoma valley there were some twenty ranch owners, living their wish—their families, servants and cowboys.

Waiting until money from their cattle had been paid, The Tiger split his band of fifty into three sections, placing them under command of Tomasso, Dato and Pulque.

"You will bring the ranch owners and their families to the colony church," he instructed his lieutenants.

"I will meet you there day after tomorrow. Be sure to fix the punchers so that they cannot attempt a rescue."

Never did church present a stranger appearance than on the day of the appointed round-up.

White-faced men, trembling women and cowering children, sat in the pews fearful of what was to happen.

And well they might be.

Entering the church with his sombrero on the back of his head, Villa swaggered to the pulpit.

"I've called you together," he announced, "because I need money.

"You have just received your pay for your cattle. I want you to bring that money to me.

"You who are ranch owners, please step up and tell me how much you can give."

But no one moved.

"Do you forget that I am Francisco Villa?" he demanded. "My time is precious. Don't make me ask you again."

But this command produced no better results than the first.

"Very well," snapped The Tiger, "if you won't do it of your own accord, I'll make you.

"Tomasso, bring in the ropes. Dato bring the branding irons."

As the men obeyed, the colonists groaned, women and children crying and shrieking.

"Now, Bepo, bring out that little girl in the first pew," he commanded.

Yelling and shrieking, the child was dragged forth, other members of the bandit gang overpowering the father and mother.

"Attach the ropes," The Tiger snapped.

Quickly they were adjusted to the child's feet and shoulders, the feet in turn being attached to the base of the pulpit.

"Ten of you take the other end and pull till I tell you to stop. Don't jerk, pull steadily."

As the bandits walked down the aisle and the slack of the rope was taken up, the father jumped to his feet.

"You're an imp of hell," he shouted, "but I cannot see my child tortured.

"I'll give you three thousand dollars."

"Now you have some sense," The Tiger exclaimed. "Go with him Dato and get the money."

As the two left the church, Villa turned to Bepo.

"Bring up that woman in the second pew on the left," he snarled.

The woman, a wife and mother, was dragged cowering to the pulpit.

"Tear off her waist and brand her back," ordered The Tiger.

Quickly his men obeyed.

As the red hot branding iron approached the white flesh of her back, the woman's husband leaped to his feet.

"Stop! And I'll give you eight thousand," he shouted.

Again the torture was prevented, and Tomasso was dispatched with the rancher to fetch the money.

One after another, Villa went through the group of colonists, and his threats of torture netted him some $35,000.

CHAPTER XXIII.

VILLA BECOMES A GENERAL.

It was shortly after this raid upon the colony at Sonoma that Villa met Raoul Madero, brother of Francisco, who had launched his revolution.

What strange bond there was between the men seems incomprehensible, so utterly unlike were they in actions, thoughts and education.

The fact remains, however, that they became the most intimate of friends.

As the Madero forces were being defeated by the Diaz troops, Raoul finally wrote a letter to his brother, acclaiming The Tiger as a hero and a military genius.

He begged him to enlist him in the cause as a general.

Naturally Francisco Madero hesitated to elevate a murdering robber, who had been hunted for fifteen years by the Rurales, from outlawry to the status of a military man.

At last, however, when his revolution was almost suppressed, Francisco Madero, willing to grasp at any straw in his desperation, sent The Tiger a commission as general in the revolutionary army.

Quickly Villa gathered the bands of malcontents and welded them into the army with which he has achieved such remarkable results.

What these are, the newspapers and magazines have described for the last three years.

But the changing of Francisco Villa from a bandit to a general has not changed his nature.

When he feels like shooting a man, he does so, regardless of who he is. He raids and plunders as in the days when he was the quarry of the Rurales. He burns and desecrates as his fancy pleases.

But his low origin, his hatred of Gringos and the aristocracy, have endeared him to his troops and to the masses, till he stands forth today as the one man in Mexico who has the paradoxical title of the people's idol and terror.

THE END.

Printed in the United States
25859LVS00005B/252